Deven Wallace shares on [...] tian family. Discovering, [...] dren's natural and God-given purposes are the highest callings as a parent. The truths outlined in her book as shared through her own purposeful discoveries will strengthen your family as it did hers! This book is a must-read!

—SHERYL BRADY
PASTOR, THE POTTER'S HOUSE NORTH

Pastor Deven Wallace has been fighting for women and their children for many years. She has been an avid advocate for helping to abolish human trafficking, is a voice for those who have no voice, and engages others to become warriors for the cause of Christ and against the things that hurt the heart of the Father. In her book *The Warrior We Call Mom* she lays out a strategy for every mom who is desperate to walk in her calling as a warrior mom to stand in the gap and make up the hedge to see the kingdom of God come and His will be done in our families. Knowledge is powerful, and this woman doesn't just give you vanilla, run-of-the-mill, worldly knowledge. She gives you knowledge through the living and breathing Word of God and revelation that has been downloaded from God to help change a culture. Be empowered, emboldened, and equipped to become that mom that every enemy from hell fears!

—JUDY JACOBS
AUTHOR, WORSHIP LEADER, COPASTOR, WARRIOR MOM

It has been almost three years since my wife and I were swept into a life-altering move of God along with our dear friends Kevin and Deven Wallace. Out of this move of the Spirit an everlasting bond was created between our two families that we never could have dreamed was possible.

I am so stirred that Yahweh has called Deven to write this book and can think of no one more anointed to do so. Deven walks in an unusual and authentic mantle that is unlike anyone I have ever been around. The greatest manifestation of this mantle is made evident through her own children. It is simply amazing to witness the love of God and the Spirit of God that fills her children. Deven's revelation concerning raising our children in the kingdom realm is life-giving and invaluable. I believe this book will be a catalyst in the lives of countless mothers who release the legacy of the kingdom into their children. Get ready! There is a generation rising, and they are filled with holy fire.

—DAMON THOMPSON
DAMON THOMPSON MINISTRIES

I have had the privilege of being a close friend of Deven's for more than a decade, and of this I am certain: she is fierce when it comes to her children. She is a woman of prayer, and she mothers, preaches, and writes from that place. The revelation and practical material in this book will change you and how you see motherhood and therefore your children. As a mother of seven I'm constantly looking for insight to be the best mom for my kids. I encourage you to read this book and then read it again! It will be life-giving to you and to your children.

—JIHAN COX
WORSHIP PASTOR, REDEMPTION LIFE CHURCH

the WARRIOR
We Call Mom

the WARRIOR We Call Mom

DEVEN WALLACE

CHARISMA
HOUSE

THE WARRIOR WE CALL MOM by Deven Wallace
Published by Charisma House
Charisma Media/Charisma House Book Group
600 Rinehart Road
Lake Mary, Florida 32746
www.charismahouse.com

Cover design by Lisa Rae McClure
Design Director: Justin Evans

Visit the author's website at www.thezionproject.net.

Library of Congress Cataloging-in-Publication Data:
An application to register this book for cataloging has been
submitted to the Library of Congress.
International Standard Book Number: 978-1-62998-728-6
E-book ISBN: 978-1-62998-729-3

Names and details of stories in this book have been changed,
and any similarity between the names and stories of individuals
described in this book and individuals known to readers is
purely coincidental.

This book contains the opinions and ideas of its author. It
is solely for informational and educational purposes and
should not be regarded as a substitute for professional medical
treatment. The nature of your child's health condition is
complex and unique. Therefore, you should consult a health
professional. Neither the author nor the publisher shall be liable
or responsible for any loss or damage allegedly arising from any
information or suggestion in this book.

While the author has made every effort to provide accurate
Internet addresses at the time of publication, neither the
publisher nor the author assumes any responsibility for errors
or for changes that occur after publication.

17 18 19 20 21 — 9 8 7 6 5 4 3 2 1
Printed in the United States of America

This book is lovingly dedicated to the four most precious and priceless gifts I have ever received: Jeremiah, Isaiah, Zion, and Judah Wallace. My heart could not be prouder of who you are becoming as I have the privilege to watch you grow and mature. I cannot wait to see the fullness of the destiny that is locked up inside of you. I love you with all of my heart, to the moon and back.

Contents

Acknowledgments

THE WELL-KNOWN OLD African proverb states that it takes a village to raise a child. I am convinced it is also true for publishing a book! This project was by no means the result of my own hands alone. I extend heartfelt gratitude and special thanks to the many "labor doulas" who stood by my side to see this goal accomplished. Above all I thank the sweet Holy Spirit for being the best friend and Counselor of this mother. I thank Him for being the greatest teacher, comfort, and guide on my crazy journey of motherhood. Any positive content of this book is the result of His infinite wisdom.

Thank you to my assistant and faithful partner in crime, Diethra Seymour. From advising to editing to being a personal cheerleader, thank you for seeing this through from start to finish. You never stopped pushing me, and you never stopped believing in me. I truly don't know if this project could have been completed without your effort and support.

I want to thank my husband and children for their patience with me during this process. Thank you, Kevin, for always releasing me to reach for the stars and obey the Lord in whatever direction He leads. Thank you, Jeremiah, Isaiah, Zion, and Judah, for encouraging me along the way, releasing me with personal stories from your lives, and carrying passion to demonstrate the kingdom of God every day! Everything I have learned about being a mother came from the hands-on experiences we have shared over the years. You are already changing the world around you, and I cannot wait to see what God unveils in each of your lives as you grow in Him. I love you and find the greatest honor and privilege of my life is being called "Mom" by each of you.

Thank you to Anna Phillips for being a spiritual mother and mentor in my life. Thank you for seeing potential in me when I was just a teenager and giving me the opportunity to see and experience God through ministry at such a stage of my life. So much of what I have learned about parenting children while being in ministry has come from watching your example over the years. I can hear your voice behind the pages of this book. Thank you for training me to be a radical follower of Christ and for continuing to equip children to be active and powerful members of the kingdom of God. My own children have been forever changed by your leadership!

Thank you to my mother and father for immersing me in ministry as a child and actually demonstrating to me from my birth how to live out the Word. I cut my teeth on the church pews, and my childhood memories are filled with being in His house. Thank you for this foundation. Thank you, Mom, for teaching me one of the best prayers I could ever pray as a mother—one you prayed over us each day: "Lord, don't let me teach my children anything You have to unteach them as adults." This has stuck with me and formed my daily decisions as a mother. Thank you for being sensitive to the Spirit and raising all of your children to be ministers in His kingdom.

Introduction

BEING A MOM in our present culture is no easy task. To say it is a challenge would be an understatement. Add the challenge of being a Spirit-filled, kingdom-minded mother with a desire and passion to raise up world changers for the glory of God. That definitely puts a "weirdo" stamp on your forehead and causes direct conflict with the flow of our culture. When I take a panoramic view of the society in which we are raising and shaping our precious little ones, I could easily become overwhelmed. Forty percent of gang members in America are under the age of eighteen.[1] Suicide is the third-leading cause of death among fifteen- to twenty-four-year-olds.[2] One in four teens will have an episode of depression while in high school, with it starting at age fourteen on average.[3] One out of five girls and one out of twenty boys are victims of sexual abuse.[4] More Americans are killed by prescription drug overdoses than heroin and cocaine combined.[5] Approximately three hundred thousand American adolescents age eighteen and under are lured into commercial sex trade every year.[6] Our parents only had to worry about pedophiles and child abductors reaching us if we walked to school or played in a bad neighborhood, but now through the advances of technology predators can find our children in the "safety" of their own bedrooms. A locked door is no longer a sufficient barrier against those who would influence and harm our children. Overwhelming pressure and responsibility are placed upon the shoulders of this generation in the name of "privilege," "freedom," or even "opportunity." Children and teens are in need of mentorship and guidance more than ever, as they are faced daily with life-altering choices, yet our families live more strained lives and parents are more preoccupied than ever. It is a deadly combination that is destroying our homes.

I am sure these facts upset you, especially if you are a mom. Your first reaction may be to cover your ears or shut your eyes and try to tune out the resonating truth that is not pleasant. We want to ignore it and avoid it. However, attempting to ignore the reality of the darkness around us does not make it vanish. This is the world we live in, and we must be shaken awake to it. This is the battle ensuing every day; our children are the goal of the conflict. This is the relentless attack and scheme of the enemy, and he will not bypass your child just because he or she is cute and innocent. The enemy is playing for keeps, preying on the unaware and the sleeping households. The only way to effectively address darkness is to acknowledge it and confront it head-on with the most powerful weapon you have: light. Turning the light on will make the darkness flee. God's truth is that light, and knowledge of His Word and His kingdom is a weapon against which darkness cannot prevail. However, if we are asleep and unaware in the spirit, we are ineffective in the authority God has given us over darkness. Just because we have access to a weapon doesn't mean we have the soberness or skill to use it. Our children could suffer defeat in the culture in which we are raising them, not because God has not given us the arsenal to be victorious but because we are not awake and aware enough to use that arsenal. According to 1 Peter 5:8, our adversary is seeking the sleeping ones. We must be sober and vigilant to resist him.

One kingdom-minded mother I know tells of how the

Spirit of the Lord spoke to her from a scene in the classic *Lord of the Rings* trilogy. She watched the onslaught of the enemy in the battle of Helm's Deep against families that had taken refuge in a fortress there. The enemy's army was so great and the village army was so small that the only way to protect the children was to arm them. As a result they placed heavy armor upon the young boys and gave them sharpened swords. As the scene unfolded before this mother and her young boys, they could see the fear and confusion reflected on the faces of the children in the movie because they had not been prepared for battle before this moment of desperation. The mother's youngest son cried out, "Momma, it's not fair that they have to fight like that." It seemed so unfair, and the armor was so bulky upon them, but it was a time and scenario when the battle was so crucial that everyone was needed. Exemption was not possible if survival was to be achieved.

We are at that time in the kingdom. The last-days outpouring prophesied in Joel 2 does not just target the old or the young, nor just male or female. This outpouring is for all of God's creation. This also means the warfare accompanying this outpouring is for everyone: old and young, male and female. This is an hour when our children are involved in the battle whether or not we want them to be. The option is not exemption or participation. There are no draft dodgers in the kingdom. The choice is whether or not we will prepare them with the skill and the weaponry to overcome. They have been surrounded, and it is our job not only to equip them with the spiritual weapons they need for victory but also to train them to use these weapons effectively and efficiently before they enter the heat of battle. I don't want my children to feel uncomfortable with the sword of the Spirit in their hands, and I don't want the breastplate of righteousness to feel too big for their chests. My children as well as the rest of this present generation need to know who their God is and who they are in Christ. They must be armed with the Word and with the knowledge of how to move heaven in prayer. We must train them not to be distracted by the diversions of the enemy around them but to passionately pursue God now, even in their youth. They should shape the culture without the culture shaping them.

There is nothing I find more annoying than the sound of a buzzing alarm clock on a cold and dark morning to wake me from my peaceful slumber. Monday mornings to me are the absolute most irritating time. The buzzing sound may begin as gentle and soft, but it is purposed to grow louder and more irritating the longer it is ignored. It is not meant to be pleasant and soothing, or else it would not accomplish its goal. The sound of an alarm is meant to be sudden and disturbing, demanding a reaction. The buzzing is a redundant message, repeating itself over and over and over, repetitive and strong, until its desired response is achieved. That is the nature of an alarm. It is not our enemy but our friend, even though we beat it mercilessly at times for an additional moment of rest. The alarm keeps us from missing the opportunities and appointments of the day. It prevents us from sleeping through what we cannot afford to miss. Alarms keep us on time, and even though we don't enjoy waking up to an alarm, we would suffer immensely without it. An alarm is a necessary irritant that we should actually be thankful for.

This is what God designed the voice of the prophet to be to His church. It is like the buzzing of an alarm. It is meant to be strong, clear, and repetitive until a response or reaction occurs. It may begin with a soft and gentle reminder, but if it is ignored, its message will grow louder and stronger.

The voice of the prophet is not designed to be ignored, and it demands a response. It is meant to shake us from a state of spiritual slumber and alert us to the current time in the kingdom. It is not easily ignored and is certainly not meant to soothe us back to a place of complacency. It is meant to wake us so we don't miss the opportunities of the kingdom of God and don't oversleep through divine appointments on God's calendar for our lives. We may not like the voice, but we must embrace its sound. Prophetic messages are necessary; they become like a compass of direction as God guides us to the direction and map of His kingdom. It is the mercy of God to set off an alarm for His people, and it is the mercy of God that releases the voice of the prophet to declare His will and agenda. It is the voice of the prophet that confronts a generation in complacency and spiritual slumber. Prophets such as Haggai, Habakkuk, Isaiah, and Jeremiah were used by God to sound the alarm in the nation of Israel. Let us not be like the children of Israel and ignore the alarm of God in this hour.

The world in which we live is in need of this prophetic alarm right now. More importantly the church itself is in need of a prophetic alarm. Just recently I visited an incredible life-size replica of Noah's ark with our church's school. An entire section of the museum inside was dedicated to artistic depiction of the state of humanity prior to the Flood. The depravity of the culture and the immanent darkness could be felt. In one of the artistic displays a phase-by-phase progression of the demise of humanity was explained, and I was shocked to see that the seven major categories of depravity that led to the need for the Flood were common issues we are seeing in our world today. Violence, sexual perversion, governmental corruption, religious corruption, polygamy, the disintegration of family, and giants ruling the land were just a few mentioned. Doesn't this sound all too familiar? In the days of Noah, the Bible says, people were eating and drinking while destruction was headed their way (Matt. 24:38–39). They were unaware and deaf to the voice of God, their maker. Their senses had been numbed, their spirits were corrupted, and they were blind to the consequences of their actions. They were asleep. God anointed Noah to declare His word, yet they mocked him. His voice became an alarm to irritate them, yet they refused to heed his words. Their response to that alarm sealed their fate.

Then, as the Messiah came onto the scene in the era of the New Testament, we find that the world again was ignorant and unaware of the heart of the Father. Oblivious to the kingdom calendar being fulfilled around them, people's spirits had been rocked to sleep by religion, and they were blind to the salvation that was right in front of them. Their appointment with a divine visitation from heaven was upon them, yet Jesus wept over them because many were sleeping through their moment. In His love and mercy God sent an alarm ahead of Him, the voice crying out like a trumpet in the wilderness—the prophet named John, who came in the spirit and power of Elijah; the camel-hair-wearing, locust-eating young man who would awaken a remnant and convict the complacent (Mark 1:1–4; Luke 1:17). He was the necessary predecessor of Christ Himself. Yet as in the case of Noah before him, many ignored or even mocked the message of John the Baptist. Again, their response to his alarm sealed their fate.

As we quickly approach the return of the Messiah, we find ourselves back in the same cycle humanity was in during the days of Noah and in the days of Christ: the sleep cycle. Matthew 24:37 says that as it was in the days of Noah, so it would be again in the days of the coming of Christ. A generation, a culture, is oblivious to its own destiny—partying instead of preparing, feasting instead of fasting, sleeping instead of praying. It is clouded by the lullaby of selfishness and greed, and it is swaddled in the cloak of religion, blind to its coming destruction. In Luke 17:26–27 Christ warned us it would be this way. As in His first appearance on the earth, when the spirit of Elijah echoed through the voice of John, so it will be in this generation. It is time for awakening, and that requires an alarm. That requires a John the Baptist crying out in the wilderness. Luke 1:17 lets us know that the alarm John the Baptist encapsulated was more than just a man; it was the spirit of awakening. It was the spirit of Elijah. I believe this spirit can come upon a whole generation. It will not be just one voice but an army of voices that will become the trumpet and warning to this generation. I believe our children can be that voice. Like John, they can awaken our world by first awakening His church.

The assignment of awakening the church starts in the comfort of our own homes; true awakening begins there. It does not begin in the aisles and at the altars of megachurches but in the revival and restoration of Christ at the center of the Spirit-filled family. The spirit of Elijah, which was on the life of John, should blanket not only this generation but also moms and dads, and it should directly affect the way we parent. It takes the whole house. Both Zechariah and Elizabeth were awakened before they could ever effectively parent their son, John. The Bible tells us that one of the assignments of the Spirit is to turn the hearts of parents, specifically fathers, to the children and the children to the fathers (Mal. 4:6). The healing and strengthening of the family unit will strengthen the church. God knows a strong kingdom is built upon strong families. This is why the family unit, our marriages, and our children are being attacked so forcefully. When we see revival within our families, we will, in turn, see revival in our nation and our world!

The spirit of the antichrist is the opposing force of the true Messiah, Jesus Christ, and the advancement of His kingdom. The spirit of the antichrist, which John already declared in 1 John 4:3 was in operation in the earth, doesn't just target mainstream preachers; it is assaulting our homes. Even 2 Timothy 3:2 states that one of the characteristics of the perilous times of the last days would be children who are disobedient to their parents and who would operate in lawlessness. As I look across the landscape of our nation, at the recent riots in the streets and protests at some of our colleges and universities, I see a spirit of lawlessness that could be linked to a root of disobedience at home. That scripture also says that the generation at the time of the return of Christ will be lovers of themselves, or selfish. This is what I call self-idolatry. This obsession with self and elevation of self over others is seen in our culture's obsession with social media outlets and even the selfie phenomenon. We are addicted to ourselves and to creating an image of ourselves that we have designed as our own reality. The culture that is attempting to influence our children and our homes is directly aligning itself with the warnings of Scripture. It is clear that the battle zones of the last days reach beyond just the church house and extend to your house; the spirit of the antichrist is attacking our families.

What is the answer? What will awaken the church to rise up and shine in this dark hour? The answer is the voice of a prophetic generation that will not compromise or settle for anything less than God's kingdom here on the earth. What will empower this generation to lift its voice like a trumpet and cry out as John the Baptist did? The initiator will be an outpouring and demonstration of God's glory and power upon our children. Even in the womb John the Baptist was filled with the Holy Spirit. He had a face-to-face encounter with the power and presence of God in a nonconventional way and at an abnormally young age. That encounter established him and set him apart. It ruined him for the good, forever. This is what this generation needs and what our prayers as mothers should cry out for. Our babies need a life-changing, face-to-face encounter with the Holy Spirit of God that will ruin them forever from being satisfied by religious systems and set them apart as a prophetic voice of the Almighty. O God, let this awakening begin by an outpouring of Your Spirit upon Your church again! This outpouring will not just stop with our babies; it should blanket our entire families. Acts 2:2 lets us know that when the Holy Spirit fell, the Spirit filled the whole house, not just one room and not just a few select individuals. He consumed the whole place and everyone in it! This is the desire of God and the nature of the Holy Spirit even today. He wants to consume your family with His glory. In this hour the Holy Spirit wants to fill your whole house!

Chapter One
KINGDOM-MINDED MOTHERS

>>>————————•

Becoming a mother was possibly the greatest transition of my life as a young woman. Kevin and I were married when I was only nineteen, and just a few short months after we celebrated our first wedding anniversary, we also celebrated the first birthday of my eldest son, Jeremiah. Everything his dad and I know about parenting came through time with him. He was our guinea pig, and we learned more from our mistakes than we did with our successes. I was the typical hover mother and germophobe. We went to the doctor every time Jeremiah sneezed, and I never left him with a babysitter. Control was security to me, and I truly thought my personal life had to cease in order for me to be a good mother. My identity became wrapped up in my child, which is a mistake so many mothers make. I was Jeremiah's mom first, Kevin's wife second, then God's daughter last. My daily decisions revolved around this mentality. Just when it seemed that I was finally finding a daily normal in my life as a first-time mommy, I found out I was expecting again! When Jeremiah was somewhere around six months of age, I discovered that Isaiah was on his way into the world. With two little ones born so closely together combined with a new pastorate that Kevin and I had been assigned, my life was truly overwhelming personally, and I felt myself turning into a robot. I lived a performance-minded, task-centered existence and lost all sight of who God had created me to be. It felt as if life was passing me by and I would never catch up. I had never experienced such unspeakable joy as I did in being a parent, but somehow this alone could not satisfy my soul. Something was crying out from within me, but I felt as if my soul and spirit were suffocating. To some of you, these thoughts and emotions of motherhood are foreign, but to others I know I am writing what you have been afraid or unable to voice in your journey. Some of you have lived under the same lie I did, and that lie is this: I thought I had to lay my future and dreams and calling on an altar in the name of motherhood, and that somehow made me more holy and righteous as a mother. Even greater, I bought the lie that this was best for my children.

This leads me to the life-changing encounter I had with the Spirit of God shortly after the birth of my daughter, Zion. She was our third child and was born during a particularly hectic season of growth and transition in our lives. She was such a precious gift to our family and to me personally, but her birth brought to light such a longing and searching for clarity and identity in my own heart and life. Our children are not just gifts, but also they are purposeful agents of light who expose the truth of our own hearts. They bring out the best and the worst in us and seem to sharpen us where we are weak. Zion's birth was the beginning of a life-changing, God-ordained transition in my heart and thinking.

At this point I enjoyed motherhood more than any other God-given assignment in my life. I had managed the best that a young pastor's wife of a growing church could with my two precious boys, but something seemed to malfunction in my ability to adjust and manage after the birth of my third child. Maybe it was because Kevin and I were outnumbered, but I could not seem to get my life together. There is no returning to normal after having a baby! A new normal must be defined. The sooner a mother comes to grips with this reality and finds the joy and excitement of a new normal instead of grieving over what has been, the sooner anxiety, depression, and fear will leave.

MINISTRY, MARRIAGE, AND MOTHERHOOD

I was up early one morning feeding Zion and sitting in our home office really wrestling with God in a time of prayer. I was complaining, asking questions, and searching my soul. I knew that God had placed a call on my life that I was not yet fulfilling completely. Add to that the frustration of feeling as if I was failing in my responsibilities as a mother, pastor's wife, and copastor. I knew that my efforts in my call to shepherd our people were falling short as I tried to play the balancing act of home and ministry. If I couldn't even fill that role effectively and manage my home, how could I ever reach the nations, as God had so clearly spoken to my heart as a young teenager? Becoming a mother was so personally fulfilling in my life, but the Lord still allowed a measure of unsettledness to remain in my heart because motherhood was not the end of my journey, or even a parking lot where I could just stop and rest for a while. He was not calling me to be only a wife and mother; I had a role to fill as His daughter—a calling He had given me when I was just a child with no husband or children—and He placed that call on my life even when He saw the gift of family coming in the future. The added blessings of husband and children did not revoke the call of God on my life. These blessings were not hindrances to this call, but they were purposed to be enhancements. They were never meant to cause conflict or competition with that call; they were all meant to complement it. The call of God upon my husband and myself was also upon our children, and if we were anointed for a specific purpose, they shared in that anointing and call.

I found myself desperately stuck in something I now call "the devil's triangle." I am not talking about the Bermuda Triangle, although the risks are very similar. The Bermuda Triangle is a region in the western part of the North Atlantic Ocean in which several ships and aircraft have "mysteriously" disappeared. I remember hearing stories as a child about the Bermuda Triangle, about how navigation systems would stop functioning and ships and aircraft would never be heard from or sighted again. This truth can be seen in the Spirit, and the devil's triangle is an area of life that many women enter, and during their time there their navigation systems of destiny and calling stop functioning properly. Because of that, identity is lost, and these women seem to never be able to find themselves again. This high-risk triangle of life has three legs to it: ministry, marriage, and motherhood. It is the balancing act where the responsibility of being the helpmate and wife; the call to be the caretaker, teacher, and shaper of another human being; and the personal call of God to fulfill our purpose and assignment on the earth as His daughter seem to converge. This triangle has been constructed for so many women, yet many never survive it. Somewhere in the middle of the balancing act we lose them on the radar of life, and they seem to spiral out of control.

I was right in the middle of this triangle, and in many ways I had already checked out from the world outside of that triangle. I seemed to lose contact with anyone and everyone who didn't fit in that zone of responsibility, and I was desperately lost and imbalanced in the middle. Ineffectiveness was all around me, and I was spiraling out of control. I had my priorities out of order, and that was certain death in this season of life. I forgot to be daughter first so that the rest would fall into place. It was on this particular morning, when I was feeding Zion while the rest of my family slept, that the Lord began to unveil to me that this stormy season was actually ordained by Him. He had actually led me right in the middle of this triangle, but I would survive and live to tell about it, and I would expose the enemy's assignment within this triangle so other moms could not only survive but also thrive in waters that are difficult to navigate.

As I was praying and crying before the Lord with my precious daughter cradled in my arms, I had an open vision that morning right there in my office. I felt disconnected from anything purposeful in the kingdom and stuck behind diapers, baby bottles, and spit-up. I was hardly able to even sit through a church service in its entirety. Yet that morning God opened up a picture of the kingdom to me, an inexperienced young mother. He met me right where I was, and when no one else seemed to see me, He did. I think the spirit realm operates much like the dream realm. You can see and hear so much in such a short amount of time. You can dream a whole day's worth of activities in just a ten-minute nap. That is what happened during this open vision.

RECOGNIZING THE STRATEGY OF SATAN'S ATTACK

What I saw that day in just a matter of moments is hard to capture in words. Somehow before me I saw the thoughts and plans of the enemy. He was being exposed to me. I saw the enemy's desire to destroy the rising generation, and I saw him desiring to destroy my children. I felt his hatred toward them and saw his obsession with methodical destruction—subtle

15

and crafty plans to contaminate and destroy the kingdom by destroying them. Honestly that wasn't a huge surprise to me because I had grown up working in children's ministry. I had heard countless sermons and declarations about how the enemy desired to take the next generation and destroy our seed.

On this day, however, I saw a twist that no one had ever revealed to me. I saw the focal point of the enemy's target that day, and it wasn't just aimed at my babies; it was aimed at me as a mother. He was focused on all mothers, especially the godly ones. He saw them as the obstacle in the way of his plans. I saw him begin to send attack after attack directly at mothers. I saw mothers wrapped in a cloak of depression as they were feeding their babies at home, mothers in their minivans with frustration upon their faces and stress upon their shoulders, their eyes exhausted and empty. I saw mothers crying (as I was) in the early hours of the morning, fighting a loneliness so real I could almost touch it. The enemy was watching them and plotting his attack. His plan was to destroy them from the inside out. He wanted to stress, depress, distract, and wear down those who were shaping the next generation. The heavy hands of the mothers were in his way, so he wanted to weary them and keep them occupied with other things so that a door could be opened for his destructive plans. The Lord began to speak to me that many in the kingdom had begun to recognize the enemy's attack upon the next generation, but few recognized the enemy's strategy. Even the church was at times overlooking the ones who were under heavy attack. The world recognizes that the hand that rocks the cradle rules the world, and the enemy knows this all too well. He was targeting the hand that rocks the cradle. He was targeting the mothers of the next generation because he knew that if he could destroy and divert them, he could take their seed.

Something rose up in me at that moment that I cannot fully articulate. A fight rose up in me that has never left my spirit. I began to realize as I was lying on my office floor crying and feeling ineffective and helpless that I was doing in the moment exactly what the enemy wanted me to do. That was exactly what he wanted me to feel. He had been targeting me to destroy me, and he was doing the same to many mothers around the world. He wanted to disconnect me from my God-given purpose in the kingdom for fear I would raise my children to walk in their destiny alongside me. He feared me modeling my call before them. He fears all mothers who are engaged in the kingdom and who train their children to follow. We as mothers are actually a threat to him—not because we may preach great sermons or travel as missionaries around the world in this season of our lives, but because what we are doing has the potential to be just

The Lord began to speak to me that many had begun to recognize the enemy's attack upon the next generation, but few recognized the enemy's strategy.

as effective as, if not more effective than, evangelistic crusades. I was shaping the next generation in my home. I was forging a weapon in my arms, quietly but faithfully. And as a mother I would be willing to fight to my last dying breath to protect the seed that had been entrusted to me. I was the one standing between the enemy and the future.

His strategy against me was not to openly make his presence known and try to come and physically take my child. There are not enough demons in hell that could physically fight against a determined and protective Spirit-filled mother. His strategy was crafty and subtle; it was called self-destruction. If he could just get in my mind and emotions, he could get to my child. If he could just get me off focus and distracted, he could steal from me. If he could just oppress and depress me, he could keep me from shaping a weapon of mass destruction in my home. If he could contaminate my thinking, destroy my identity, and shake my faith, I would, in turn, do his work for him in my child. When this revelation hit me, I had a personal awakening!

Children themselves are weapons against the enemy, even from birth. David said, and Christ restated, that "out of the mouths of babes and nursing infants You have ordained strength because of Your enemies, to silence the enemy and the avenger" (Ps. 8:2; see also Matt. 21:16). The word *ordained* means "anointed" or "appointed." It was the day of His entry into Jerusalem that Christ repeated this as the children cried in the streets, "Hosanna" (Matt. 21:15). His entry was preceded by a young generation of prophetic praisers who were anointed and appointed for a prophetic moment that history would record. They silenced those who would speak from the spirit of the antichrist and discredit Christ as Messiah. They declared what could not be seen with the physical eye, only with prophetic insight. I declare Christ's return will be no different. As He makes His triumphant return, He will be preceded by a generation of young prophetic praisers. This group of children will release a sound that will silence the spirit of the antichrist and declare the holiness of God. They will war through their sound, and the enemy knows this. He knows the power of their praise, and he is determined to silence them before they silence him.

His strategy is to silence this generation by silencing the

mothers. As I travel and minister around the world, never have I seen more mothers who are distracted by goals and pressures that have no eternal value. So many mothers are living on medication just to find feelings of happiness again, as they are attacked by depression and anxiety. In churches I see mothers with tear-filled eyes walking the halls and sitting in nursery rooms, wondering if they will ever survive this challenging season and if anyone even knows they actually made it to church that day.

This book is about awakening mothers, the silent warriors. It is about sounding the alarm to the army that the enemy fears the most: Spirit-filled, kingdom-minded mothers!

They have lost their praise and their song. Their silence has weakened their ability to fight. They have exchanged their armor, a garment of praise, for a garment of heaviness and despair. Silent mothers model silence and mold silent children.

In the fast pace of our society we have at times failed to give proper significance and honor to those who are truly shaping society. It's not government programs or educational programs or even church programs that make the greatest impact on a child's life. It is the shaping of a mother and father that molds a child with the greatest significance. This book is about awakening mothers, the silent warriors. It is about sounding the alarm to the army that the enemy fears the most: Spirit-filled, kingdom-minded mothers!

The enemy may have attempted to lure you to sleep, woman of God, but I am praying that an alarm is sounding so loudly right now that you cannot ignore it or push the sleep button. This is an alarm that mandates immediate action. As Isaiah

52:2 says, we must rise up and shake the dust off ourselves. Get up, woman of God, and realize you have a great assignment to shape the seed with which you have been entrusted. We can change the culture around us and shape the future of the kingdom of God just by helping to raise up and release a prophetic generation. We can train an army that will shape the culture without the culture shaping it. However, we as mothers must first resist the molds of the culture ourselves.

WHOM ARE YOU RAISING
UP IN YOUR HOUSE?

One child with promise and destiny can change the future of an entire nation. Just look at the lives of John the Baptist (whom we have already discussed), Samuel, Joseph, Moses, Samson...and the list goes on. They were weapons in the hand of the Lord that transformed entire nations for generations to come! Where did the battle and victory start? It was in the radical obedience and alertness of their mothers. The deliverance of Israel through Moses really started when Jochebed, his mother, released him in a basket (Exod. 2:3). The turning of Israel back to the true worship of God and the change in the political structure of that nation started with a mother named Hannah crying out at the altar of God for a child. The battle was won the day Hannah placed her precious promise from God, her baby boy, Samuel, on the doorstep of the temple and walked away empty-handed (1 Samuel 1). Israel's deliverance from the Philistines really started when Manoah's wife didn't care who made fun of her or if her son got mad at her rules. She would never cut his hair or allow him to drink the fruit of the vine. She shaped him even against his own choice at times, as God instructed her, to set him up for destiny (Judg. 13).

Who is in your house, Mom? There are women recorded throughout the Holy Bible for generation after generation to read about not because they traveled the world or received awesome degrees or had high-paying jobs. They were recorded in God's history book because they birthed children of prophetic destiny and were radically obedient and soberly aware as they shaped those children.

You could be shaping our nation's future even as you change a diaper or fold laundry. You could be impacting generations to come or shifting the tide of the kingdom just by reading the Bible at night to your children and making sure they get to the house of God, even when it's hard. You could be shaping an awakening in the world just as John Wesley's mom did when she spent time with her children every day, faithfully forming their destiny, even before anyone noticed.

It's time for us as mothers in our nation to rise up and take back what we have permitted to be taken. You are a kingdom-minded mother and an anointed warrior who will see that the enemy's plans will not prosper and that the heart of God in the earth will prevail, one child at a time. The Word of the Lord to you, Mom, is, "Arise, shine, for your light has come, and the glory of the LORD has risen upon you" (Isa. 60:1)!

I declare awakening over you to a sober awareness of the potential you have been entrusted with in this hour in the kingdom. You are called to help raise up a prophetic generation that will usher in the return of the Messiah. You are called to shape a generation that will cry out as John did and not be afraid to look and act differently than the world looks and acts. You are called to prepare the way for Messiah and help see His kingdom come here on the earth as it is in heaven. I declare every weight that has hindered you and every deception that has blinded you will be broken today in the name of Jesus. You are the devil's worst nightmare and God's secret weapon; today you awaken to your kingdom assignment. ❖

Chapter Two
THE ARROWS IN YOUR QUIVER

>>>>•————————————•►

DURING THE EARLY years of my walk with God I truly
wanted to become everything He desired and purposed for me to be. I prayed that God would make me a
vessel of honor as 2 Timothy 2:20–21 states, not just for
common use, but for special uses. I focused so much on
becoming a beautiful vessel for Him, yet in the call that
God had placed upon my life, it didn't seem as if there was
much glamour, beauty, or honor. I continually seemed to
be fighting uphill battles. As my husband and I traveled the
nation to preach, we seemed to find ourselves standing in
the valley of dry bones time and time again. God seemed
to send us to the difficult and dead places. Spiritual warfare
became part of our lives, and the assignments that God gave
to us always seemed to be resurrecting dry bones or pene-
trating thick darkness. Specifically, being a woman who was
called to preach at times lacked the glamour of the pretty
vessel I desired to be. It brought opposition and awkwardness that required divine breakthrough. I would always say
to myself as I took the pulpit to preach that I should remain
calm and just "speak" instead of "preach." However, when
the anointing would begin to flow, I was anything but calm.
A boldness and authority would arise, and I could not contain myself in a glamorous manner. The Word was truly fire
in my bones, as the prophet Jeremiah once said (Jer. 20:9).
In fact, the more I wrestled to conserve my image, the hotter

the Word would burn within me. God refused to let me fit the mold that I thought was more socially acceptable. God was not concerned with my form. He was concerned with my complete surrender to His Spirit so His power could flow through my life.

If being a woman preacher was not enough, God called me to intervene in the injustice of human trafficking. The horrific world I was immersed in was definitely no glamorous ride; it was one of warfare and rescue. It was thick darkness that took intercession, fasting, blood, sweat, and tears to make headway. There were and still are many sleepless nights and challenges. To me, my assignments have never been easy or glamorous assignments, and I wrestled with God in prayer over my identity as a vessel.

THE WARRIOR WITHIN

I had a revelation one day as I asked the Lord, "Will it always be a battle? Will it always be such a challenge? I just wanted to be a pretty vessel."

God said, "Deven, I didn't create you just to be a pretty vessel; I made you to be a weapon in My hand." There is a tremendous difference between the purpose of a vessel and the purpose of a weapon. That was the day my perspective changed, and the warrior inside of me was awakened.

Vessels are made to be filled and then used to pour out their contents. They can be polished, ornate, and pleasant to look at and receive from. They can bring refreshing. Weapons, however, are meant to protect and to destroy. They are purposed for battle, not the table. They are usually bloody, dirty, and covered with the residue of war. Weapons don't receive much downtime, and they definitely don't sit on a shelf. Weapons are meant to destroy and conquer. Beauty is not their goal. Instead, their priority is breaking down strong-holds and making way for advancement. Protection and advancement are the reasons for their creation. God was correcting the misconception I had about my identity as a vessel of His creation. He is not just a potter by the potter's wheel, as the prophet Jeremiah saw Him in Jeremiah 18, but He is also a blacksmith shaping iron and metal into fierce battle gear.

Jeremiah 51:20 states that Jerusalem is a battle-ax and a weapon of war. The Lord said He would make Jerusalem a weapon in His hand to shatter the enemy. He had forged His people into a weapon in His hand to destroy those who opposed Him. We too can be mighty weapons for the Lord!

Isaiah 54:17 is the famous text that declares "no weapon that is formed against you shall prosper," but it is verse 16 that lets us know the Lord is over the blacksmith and the forge and that He is forming weapons for Himself. It is necessary at times for the Lord to move from the potter's wheel to the iron guild to accomplish His will on the earth. You and your children can be those weapons, and that is what makes you a warrior suited for battle.

Yes, children are weapons in formation. Psalm 127:4 says that children are like arrows in the hands of a warrior! An arrow is not a toy to play with, and it is definitely not made to sit on a shelf. An arrow is a fierce weapon designed to inflict harm to its target. It is sharp, swift, and deadly. This is the imagery the Lord conveys as He reflects on the kingdom potential of children.

An arrow, however, is useless lying dormant on a table or sitting lifeless in a quiver. It has dormant potential that cannot be released until it is in the hands of a skilled warrior. It is only as good as the hands that fire it. Psalm 127:4 says, "As arrows in the hand of a *mighty warrior,* so are the children of one's youth" (emphasis added). In this verse the arrow is not enough until it is coupled with a mighty warrior. Who is that mighty warrior? That would be you!

This is God's perspective of you in the Spirit realm. He may see your children as arrows, but He sees you as the skilled warrior who holds them in your quiver. Your house is full of deadly potential, but the responsibility to release it is in your hands. In the natural you may tote a diaper bag, drive a minivan, and be an expert at bandaging "ouchies." Your neighbors and friends may not properly identify the threat you really are, but the enemy certainly does. In the realm of the Spirit, that unseen realm where God operates and the angels of the Lord move about, you are purposed and anointed to be a mighty warrior. Not only are you a protector of those in the next generation, but also you have been entrusted with the responsibility of releasing their fierce potential. You are the one who stands in between darkness and light with an arsenal at your fingertips.

There is a warrior nature inside of every mother. We may seem sweet and gentle on the outside, but see what we transform into if someone messes with our children. Then the God-given warrior-like nature rises up within us. Without a moment of hesitation a mother would take on wild beasts or armed intruders with no weaponry at all if her child was threatened. Instinct would move us beyond reasoning into warrior mode. Don't ever underestimate the fight within you, woman of God!

That is how God views a kingdom mother. When God made the first mother, Eve, He called her a helpmate (Gen. 2:18). He designed her to carry and incubate the perpetuation of life and to be a fierce protector. The word used for Eve, helpmeet, in the Hebrew text is the word *ezer*. It is not meant to be interpreted as a helper who irons and cooks, although we all know how valuable that is. This is a warrior-like term for someone who aids in battle. *Ezer* is used twenty-one times in the Old Testament, two times referring to wives and fourteen times referring to God Himself and His nature in battle![1] For example, when David cried, "I will lift my eyes to the hills, from whence cometh my help" (Ps. 121:1, KJV), that word *help* is the same word God called woman, *ezer*.

Your domestic responsibilities are noble, but they are not your identity. God decided to create you before there were dishes to wash and before the first babies were ever born! You were first formed and created with the pattern of a warrior in mind. You embody the *ezer*, or the

The enemy still fears the godly seed of a godly woman.

intervening, helping nature of God! You are to come alongside your spouse as a fellow warrior to guard each other's backs and blind spots, and you are to reign in the dominion of the kingdom of God together. You are a warrior who produces your own weapons for the kingdom. You incubate, shape, and release arrows!

It was sin that distorted this original role of woman and mother and demoted and imprisoned the one the enemy feared, the woman. The enmity was not between Adam and Satan, but Eve and Satan. Satan would fear the fruit of the womb of woman. The enemy still fears the godly seed of a godly woman. He realizes the potential of your warrior-like nature and will oppress, confuse, and distort your self-perception. He wants to continue to oppress Eve and gain dominion over her children. He wants to use your influence and your rescuing, helping nature for his kingdom instead of God's. He wants you to tear down your house for him, by your own hands of might and influence, because he knows you have been given power to build it up (Prov. 14:1).

It is the Holy Spirit who is calling for an awakening in mothers of this generation. We can no longer let the enemy steal our children. We must awaken the spiritual warrior within and go to our knees in battle. We must seek God in prayer and fasting and come out of our prayer closets with a strategy to combat the assignments of the enemy. We must rise up to the role of *ezer*, or helpmeet, and become a defender of our homes and marriages.

There is an alarm sounding in the kingdom that should alert us to battle. Our homes are the territory in dispute, and our children are the spoils of war. We cannot sit idly by and allow our culture to condition our children to walk into the traps of the enemy. You are positioned to stand in the way of darkness and become the first line of defense. Get up and get back in the fight!

Who would have ever thought of a mother or father as a warrior? That is what God expects of us as parents—not only to shape our children as weapons in His hands but also to be skilled warriors with the weapons He has entrusted to us. If we are walking below our own kingdom potential, how can we ever expect our children to hit their intended target? We must be in position and in alignment with His heart for our own lives first. Our alignment will align our seed. Then we must gain the strength to pull back our bow and have the vision to clearly see the intended target to launch our children toward success. We want them to hit their target!

UNDERSTANDING SIN

In reality, the ultimate description of sin is to miss the mark. The word *sin* in itself is an archery term. It literally was called out in archery tournaments by the judge to indicate when an arrow launched by a competitor failed to hit the middle of the bull's-eye. This is the concept of sin: to miss God's intended bull's-eye for our lives. Actions of sin that are easily identified—lying, cheating, murder, adultery—are really aimed at the same intention. The intention is to ensure you miss your destiny and purpose.

When we approach sin from this concept and teach our children to approach sin from this concept, it revolutionizes our focus. Sin is not a list of dos and don'ts from God so He can punish us if we break a rule. Sin and sinful actions are pitfalls from the enemy that will keep you from your target. Restriction from sin is not about legalism, but it is about avoiding anything that could keep you from reaching your full potential.

Sin is the weight that throws us off course and slows down our progress (Heb. 12:1). Sin is the hindrance that distracts us as warriors from remaining focused on our goal. It is the kryptonite of our souls that makes us easy targets for the enemy. Our sins not only keep us off track from our own destiny, but they also affect our ability to shape and fire our weapons; therefore our actions affect the destiny of our children. This is the weight of being a parent. Either our daily lives and choices make it easy for our children to follow God and find their purpose, or our daily lives can deter them from the Lord and cause them to wander from their God-given destiny.

Why would an arrow miss its intended destination? There are two basic reasons: faulty firing or faulty formation. Faulty firing is in the hands of the archer and cannot be attributed to the arrow itself. The responsibility of firing or releasing the arrow is upon the skill of the archer. When you view an image of an archer preparing to release the perfect shot of an arrow, you can clearly see by the form of the arms of the archer that the key is opposing force. It is the balance of opposing tension that creates the force to fire effectively. The arrow is literally suspended between intense yet balanced forces pushing forward and pulling back at the same time. This is such an accurate depiction of parenting, especially for parents of preteens and teens! The building of opposing tension at times is a sign that release is near.

In the early stages of parenting, our children are like arrows being formed and shaped for their assignments. We as parents are all the while gaining the strength and knowledge for the moment of release.

THE SEASON OF RELEASE

Not only are we being conditioned for this moment of release, but also we are conditioning our children for this moment. It seems to always be harder on the parent than it is on the child. There comes a time and season when the arrow has been shaped, and release is inevitable and quickly approaching. This is when the arrow is moved from the worktable and actually placed within the span of the bow. It is locked in and made ready, and the countdown begins. In this intense yet short period of preparation the archer is searching for and locking focus on the location of the intended target and aligning the position of the arrow. What an incredibly exciting yet sobering moment it is when we as archers in the spirit can finally see the target and can begin to turn the arrow's head in the right direction of its destiny. We don't determine the target, but we must remain sensitive to the Spirit to align with the target. It is our job to give it the force and direction to endure the journey and sustain the speed from our bow to His target. This force comes only from the balance of opposing tension: pushing forward and pulling back, both at the same time. This is the challenging balancing act of parenting a developing young adult.

Pushing forward can be demonstrated when we give more trust, more decision-making ability, more freedom, and more opportunities to our children to operate in their own set of talents and gifts, independently of our guidance. Pushing forward allows them to stretch their wings in the boundaries of our love, care, and protection. Pushing forward is watching them experience both positive and negative consequences of their actions without our immediate intervention. Pushing forward is allowing them to make choices, even bad ones, within our realm of covering. We begin to push the arrow forward and away from us to see how it might fly solo. This is an act of love called restraint. We must step back as mothers and allow our children to wrestle a bit in their own lives within the realm of safety. It is the principle of the butterfly. The struggle in the process of breaking free from the cocoon is what gives its wings strength to fly. If you have ever observed this process, you may feel a great temptation to cut or stretch the cocoon and make the process easier, but we must remember that what is easier is not always what is best. The struggle may be difficult to watch, but it is a friend and teacher.

Just to bring some added consolation to mothers of teens, the butterfly seems as if it loses its head in the process of transformation from caterpillar to butterfly. The head capsule comes off! I think every teen goes through the process of nearly losing his head in spiritual growth and development, and this makes us as parents want to lose our minds! Not only do teens' physical brains go through many chemical changes, but also their thought processes shift and change. They begin to question the world around them and even the faith you may have raised them to believe. They hopefully begin to know God as their own God and not just as the God of their parents. The Lord Himself began that face-to-face, direct relationship with Moses at the burning bush (Exod. 3). He let Moses know that He had been the God of his forefathers, but He was also his God. This is an important part of pushing forward. We must allow our children to find their burning bush moment, even if they have to wander on the mountain alone. We must let them wrestle with God and walk out their own journey of obedience. They must work out their own salvation with fear and trembling (Phil. 2:12). They cannot ride our coattails to heaven, and part of release is helping them find God for themselves. Pushing forward means letting your child seemingly lose her mind to gain the mind of Christ.

At the same time we reach a moment we must balance by pulling back. This occurs in the form of guiding, intervening, and mentoring. Pulling back means helping our children realize that trust carries responsibility, and failure in responsibility equals a relinquishing of freedom and privilege. It is intervening when their choices carry consequences of great negative impact and not allowing them to ruin their lives with immature choices or impulsive moments. Pulling back is forming realistic expectations of the maturity level and decision-making abilities of your child and giving freedom within boundaries. When pulling back, you cannot be afraid to instill boundaries when needed, being a parent more than a friend. Pulling back is not always popular, but it can be this intervention that prevents self-destruction in the life of an adolescent. Boundaries give a sense of security and are a sign that they are still held within the span of the parents' bow. Whether it be concerning unhealthy relationships or self-destructive behaviors, the truth is teenagers don't always know what is best; they sometimes need the tough love of a parent. They can be very passionate and convincing and even rope you into their self-deception, headed at times in the wrong direction, believing with all their heart that they are making right choices. Pulling back is not always appreciated, and is definitely not immediately understood, but pulling back is the responsibility of the parent to whom God has entrusted the child. Pulling back is the season when you may not be popular but you are critically needed.

During this time of opposing tension of pushing forward and pulling back, the arrow is suspended in the middle. The arrow is stretched between the tension, and both the archer and the arrow can feel it, the forces pushing forward to prepare for release and the forces pulling back to balance time and maturity until the moment is right. It is this tension that requires the most strength and patience, but it produces the force necessary to give the arrow the momentum to reach the target. This is the season that unveils all the years of training, praying, sowing, and investing. The stage of adolescence is not just a seed-sowing season of parenting; it is also a fruit-inspecting season. This is when we as parents are sometimes shocked by the fruit that appears, some negative and some positive, revealing a lifetime of seed sown.

The demand on parenting is the highest in this season. Some parents face the challenge of weariness and find it difficult to endure the struggle. They choose to fire too early or hold on too long. They may choose to completely disengage. They allow the arrow to fall to the ground because of weariness. We must condition ourselves for this moment, Mom, and this strength can only be drawn from an inner strength from the Holy Spirit Himself. There is no cookie-cutter pattern to follow for successful parenting of adolescents. The strategy needed can be as unique as the individual you are shaping. It requires unconditional love, excessive time and attentiveness, and constant communication with the heavenly Father. For some it requires the "prodigal son" type of love. For others it requires strength to not always be the best friend but to be the best mentor instead—requiring strength to trust yet also to protect, strength to trust God for the balance of pushing and pulling and waiting on His direction for the moment of release. For some it's learning the love of restraint, of not intervening when our hearts are breaking to fix everything. The strength of the warrior comes to its greatest test as she demonstrates her ability to stretch out her bow and wait for the moment of release.

God's command to release may not come at the moment that is most convenient or sensible to us. Yet we must trust Him. Elizabeth, mother of John the Baptist, may not have been ready to let her child roam the wilderness. Hannah may not have been ready to leave Samuel at the doorstep of the temple. Jochebed probably wept as she placed Moses in the basket by the river. These commands would not have made sense to the community's mothers, I am sure. I am positive these mothers were talked about and ridiculed by many. It is God, however, who knows when our children are ready, and our interference with His timing can hurt their ability to hit the target. The firing moment of every child is as unique as the child's purpose, and comparing it to others' or using human reasoning will not always line up with the plans of the Lord. It was human reasoning against the directives of the Lord that caused the fall of man to begin with and made the first created beings miss their mark! We must remember our ways are not His ways and His thoughts and ways are much higher than ours (Isa. 55:9). Listen for His release, and respond in the way we have trained our children, demonstrating immediate, complete, and radical obedience. This is what it takes to be a kingdom-minded mother. Obedience is the greatest key to success.

ARMED WITH POTENTIAL

The scariest and most uncertain moment for both the archer and the arrow (parent and child) is that moment when the tension has created the force needed, the alignment is in place, and the arrow is released to leave the safety of the bow to become airborne. Being airborne is the moment when the arrow is no longer in the hand of the archer but has not yet reached the center of the target. The arrow is suspended in midair, traveling at a very rapid and potentially dangerous speed. In this critical moment you as the parent are no longer in control. It's between the Lord and your precious child alone. All you can do is hold your breath, wait, watch, and pray.

When an arrow is released from the bow, it will actually waver in the air due to the force of release, the shaft wobbling and bending. However, if the arrow has been shaped correctly in formation, it will even out and return to its shape and travel in the direction in which it was aimed. This brings new meaning to the verse "Train up a child in the way he should go, and when he is old he will not depart from it" (Prov. 22:6). The phrase "train up" is similar to the idea of shaping a child, and "the way he should go" is the intended direction toward the target. If proper training occurs early in life, there is a promise we can hold on to that when release happens, no matter how the wind blows or the force of release affects the arrow, it will eventually return to its original form. "When he is old" lets us know as mothers that it may not be an immediate return, and some wavering and wobbling may occur, but it will go in its intended direction.

The wavering of a literal arrow takes just a few short moments of time, but those few moments can seem like eternity. All stability seems to have been lost. At that point it is all up to the wind. Those few milliseconds reveal a lifetime of training and conditioning, both of the archer and the arrow. It is the same in the spirit. When the Lord directs us to release our children, we are not releasing them to travel through life alone. The Holy Spirit is the One to whom we release them. He is the wind. It is the wind of the Spirit that will carry our arrows and keep them on course. The Holy Spirit is the ultimate guide and momentum-producing force. He will ultimately lead our children and guide them into all truth (John 16:13). Just as Christ left His disciples in the hand of the Holy Spirit, so we as parents must experience this release. God released His only Son into the world to hit His target, so He understands the emotions of release. God does not ask us to abandon them or leave them comfortless, as Christ said in John 14. We leave them in the hands of the Holy Spirit, and we listen to His instructions for them. We do all that we can do as parents, and then we must trust the leading of the wind. Trust the Holy Spirit, trust what you have sown, and master the season of release with supernatural peace.

As mothers and spiritual archers we must walk in awareness of the danger of misfiring our arrow. If we are off focus or cannot see the target clearly, we place our arrows in a danger zone. There could be obstructions or distractions, or we could be aiming completely in the wrong direction. You can have the finest arrow and the strongest arm, but if you aim in the wrong direction, the bull's-eye is not even a possibility. In fact, you could miss the target altogether and cause your child to become a lost arrow.

As a pastor I see many lost young people so far from the plans of God for their lives because their archers had their own agendas in mind. The parents steered and aimed in the opposing direction of the place that God had prepared for the young adults because they were not surrendered to the leading of the Holy Spirit. I see this so many times in the lives of "PKs" (pastors' kids) or ministry kids whose parents intentionally either steer them away from kingdom work or force them to it, depending upon their own personal experience. They forget to seek the Lord for the direction of their children. These young ladies and men are unfulfilled and left lost somewhere between the bow and the target, spending most of their days searching for purpose instead of fulfilling it. As mothers we must remove all personal agenda from the training and release of our babies. We must remind ourselves that they are God's children before they are ours. We don't make the target; we simply release the arrows. We don't write their story; we simply turn the pages. It is sometimes difficult to discern between God's plans and our own dreams for our children, but living a life of daily surrender before the Lord and staying in His Word will divide between what is soul and what is Spirit. We must be attentive to the hearts of our children and identify the God-given gifts and desires He has placed within them, even if those desires and gifts don't match our own or are not what we are comfortable with. Strong arrows in the hands of weary warriors won't go the distance. Sharpened arrows in the hands of blind or distracted warriors won't penetrate the target. A prophetic generation in the hands of a weak, distracted, or wrongly motivated father, mother, or mentor will not be successful against the kingdom of darkness. We have to remember that these arrows are God's gift, not our possessions. He has the instruction manual for their growth and success. Abba knows best.

As mothers we must realize that the possession of arrows identifies us as potential threats to the enemy, whether we see that when we look in the mirror or not. The enemy sees someone armed with potential. However, just because arrows identify us and give us the appearance of warriors doesn't mean we are qualified to be warriors. We must be accountable to God for living a life passionate for Him and His kingdom. We must submit our lives daily to the training required to be skilled warriors in the kingdom of God. We must be strong, vigilant, sober, and focused. We cannot afford to be sleepy, complacent, or kingdom couch potatoes. We must allow the Holy Spirit to train our hands to war and our fingers to battle (Ps. 144:1). Then we must model such conditioning and training to our children. This strategy comes directly from constant communication with God in prayer and intercession. That is where you receive battle plans, and that is where you are sharpened as a warrior. The arrows in our quivers can be made fierce and dangerous or faulty and ineffective by how we steward our own lives. Don't be what prevents your arrow from reaching its intended destination. Be a force behind its purpose and a propellant to its destiny. You are a warrior, woman of God. Awaken to the assignment before you, and shake the kingdom of darkness with the arrows you have been given!

I declare an awakening to you, Mother—an awakening from apathy, complacency, and spiritual slumber. I declare a restoration of God's original plan over you, and I break off every lie the enemy has utilized to bind you and hinder you from taking your place in the kingdom. I pray the warrior inside of you would rise up and your hands would build your house to withstand every storm of the enemy. Your fingers have been trained for battle, and may you have the grace to release your children to their kingdom destiny. ❖

Chapter Three
BE LOOSED TO LEAD

>>>>>>——————————————

Y OU ARE A leader. All moms are meant to be leaders. A
leader by definition is simply one who guides, especially
by advancing. It can even mean to move someone in a direction by taking the person by the hand. I can see that image
now—a daily activity of a mom and her young child, walking
hand in hand. Those little hands are always reaching up to
his mom to be led. It is in the spirit as it is in the natural.
They are reaching for someone, for you, to lead them as they
grow. But where are you going? Where are you leading them?

THE SIGNIFICANCE OF MOTHERHOOD

I personally believe moms are the most significant leaders
in our nation and world. William Ross Wallace said, "The
hand that rocks the cradle is the hand that rules the world."[1] I
believe he was a wise man for recognizing the significance of
motherhood and the ability of mothers to influence the world
even from the boundaries of the home. While some leaders are
leading business deals, company mergers, or building projects,
moms are leading the most important and valuable group in
this nation—the next generation. You will not necessarily get
paid for what you do and will probably never get an award
for your leadership performance or accomplishments, but rest
assured, heaven knows the importance of those who mold the
rising generation of boys and girls. Hell also takes note. The

enemy knows the power of the influence of a godly mother, and that is why he has chosen to target mothers so fiercely. We hold the future of our nation and the kingdom in our arms.

The most impressionable and moldable years of a child's life are from birth to five years. During those first five years of programming and imprinting, who is the individual who is near to the child the most? The mother! In fact, in biblical times it was normal for a child to not be weaned until age five![2] Those important years are purposely designed for children to spend next to their greatest influence and leader—their mother—in a very intimate connection. It is why Moses never bowed to Egypt; it is why Samuel never bowed to religious corruption. From birth through weaning, the most impressionable years of their lives, they were face-to-face with godly mothers. The seeds planted during those years could never be uprooted by man or Satan. We automatically think Satan wakes up daily to attack world leaders, leading television preachers, or prominent church leaders of the day. I have come to notice, however, that he has launched a vicious attack on the most threatening individuals to his dark kingdom—kingdom-minded, Spirit-filled mothers.

EMBRACING YOUR IDENTITY

The morning I was feeding Zion in my office, I had a wake-up call that did not just come from the hungry cry of my daughter; the vision God gave me that day was a wake-up call in my spirit. God set my house in order starting with me. He first addressed me as a daughter. He took me to my knees in the vision, and then He began to unveil to me the fullness of His calling upon my life. At 5:30 a.m., when the world was asleep, He wasn't. He noticed me and heard my cry, and He confirmed His call over my life.

What I saw in the Spirit was more than I could reveal in the pages of a book, and it was more massive than my hands could ever accomplish. True vision from God is always bigger than what you can accomplish alone. I saw the fulfillment of what I am beginning to see now in the ministry of The Zion Project. My mission and anointing is to see broken women set free and empowered by the Spirit, both in the natural and in the spirit. When I saw the vision, I began to wrestle fear. As I was looking at my baby daughter, I said to the Lord, "How? How can I do this with kids? I won't leave them, and I won't fail them. I can't do all this." The Lord took me to the words of Matthew 10:37–39: "He who loves son or daughter more than Me is not worthy of Me.... He who finds his life will lose it, and he who loses his life for My sake will find it." The words pierced me to my core. As I looked at my baby girl, I had to surrender all over again to my Lord. My children and my family could not come before Him. I had to love Him first.

He said to me that my identity could not be limited to being a mother. My identity first was as His daughter. If I was an obedient and faithful daughter to Him, I would be the "perfect" mother I was striving to be. He let me know that day that if I sought Him first and loved Him first, He would honor His word. If I sought His kingdom first, He would add all things unto me (Matt. 6:33). If I put Him first, He would take care of my babies.

I realized in that moment that I had begun to lose my identity as God's daughter in my identity as a mother. My children needed me to cook for them, dress them, and be an excellent mother, but they also needed to see me love and obey my Father. If all my efforts went to being a mother, I would fall short. However, as His daughter I would have God's help as a mother. His grace would go further than my efforts could ever go. That day I committed to radical obedience to Him and His call on my life, even when it was difficult as a mother. God has been faithful to His word, to my family, and to me. All I had to do was obey, and He did so much more than I could have accomplished on my own. Obedience aligned our house for supernatural blessing. More than homemade bread and a squeaky clean house, my children needed to see me be passionate for the kingdom so they could come alongside me as I fulfill my destiny. I love nothing more than polishing my domestic skills, but when God calls, I am not afraid to let go of my perfectionism and put His kingdom first. I pray I have led my children to do the same!

THE KINGDOM OF GOD IS HAPPENING RIGHT IN YOUR HOME!

Not only did God set me straight as His daughter and let me know I had to let go of some of my obsessive parenting, but He also corrected my identity as a mother. He unveiled the lies of the enemy that I had been consuming hook, line, and sinker. My life was not unnoticed, and the world was not passing me by. The kingdom of God was happening right in my home! Heaven was noticing me and considered my daily mission to be valuable. God began taking me through the women in Scripture who were named with great honor not because of their business success or even their ministry success but because of their obedience as mothers. These women literally changed nations and forever impacted

If I put Him first, He would take care of my babies.... My children needed me to cook for them, dress them, and be an excellent mother, but they also needed to see me love and obey my Father.

the kingdom because each gave birth to one prophetic child and followed the instructions of the Lord as a steward of that gift. These mothers did not conform to popular opinion or to what all the other mothers were doing. They listened to heaven and obeyed, and because of that they made history.

God values motherhood and sees each mother as a kingdom leader and anointed vessel. He is there for the night feedings and aware of the dirty diapers. He cares about temper tantrums and postpartum depression. I discovered the Holy Spirit is on assignment with me every day as I parent to help me mold dangerous weapons against the kingdom of darkness. My home is not a prison for me; it is an arsenal for the armies of heaven. I am a maker of arrows, not a weak link in society. The enemy lied to me to try to intimidate me. He tried to devalue me because he was terrified of me. He knows from history that his enemy is the mother, so he worked very hard to make sure I never figured that out. This is the strategy of Satan. Broken, deceived, and depressed mothers produce broken, deceived, and depressed children. Where the mother is headed, the children follow. Satan was directly attacking me, along with godly mothers across the globe, in order to wound and defeat the next generation of prophetic voices. I broke free that day and received the truth of my assignment.

My children are not in the way of my calling; they are a part of it. They are anointed alongside their father and me to change the world with the message of the kingdom. Once I knew this, our home became holy training ground, and I began to take every moment to shape my children to impact the world around them. They are full of potential, and it is my job to unleash and unlock it. I determined that day that I could change the world from my living room and my kitchen table!

JOINT CALLING, JOINT DESTINY

The Lord instructed me to expose this assignment of the enemy. The Lord desired to strengthen the mothers, break off deception and fear, and arm them with the strategy for battle. He shifted my focus to center not just around the next generation but also around the leaders of the next generation. He said to renew intimacy in prayer among mothers and train them to fast and pray and follow the leading of the Holy Spirit. He said for me to train my ears to hear and train my heart to obey.

Your greatest weapons are prayer and radical obedience. Don't settle for the lie of the enemy or the depression that lies can bring! Heaven sees you, Mom, and heaven is on your side. You are a force to be reckoned with! Run hard after Him and the kingdom, and your children will do the same. Don't just run off and leave them, but take them by the hand and bring them with you. This is a family affair. The priesthood and service of God was always a family affair. From the Old Testament until now the whole family of the priest helped in the service of the temple. You and your babies are anointed for this hour! The Holy Spirit will empower you for your assignment, and you don't have to live overwhelmed. You are on the front lines of battle in the kingdom right now, even if the enemy doesn't want you to realize it. The struggle you have endured and the pressure you have been under aren't just your hormones or your emotions; there is a spiritual layer to what you have been experiencing. You cannot fight the spiritual battle with carnal weapons, so you must pull out the spiritual armor the Lord has equipped you with. No medication can correct perspective or erase the lies of the enemy. Only the power of the Holy Spirit can truly set you free and give you the correct focus.

In Matthew 21:2 we find the familiar passage recording Jesus preparing to ride in to Jerusalem for what we historically call Palm Sunday. It was a day prophesied about in the records of the prophets and can even be seen in Zechariah 9:9. The Messiah would ride into Jerusalem on a humble donkey as the people would declare His messiahship. In Matthew 21:2 we see Jesus give instructions to His disciples to get the choice vessel He would ride upon. He said, "Go over into the village opposite you, and immediately you will find a donkey tied, and a colt with her. Untie them and bring them to Me." I knew my whole life that Jesus rode on a donkey. I had seen this scene of Jesus riding victoriously into Jerusalem on a donkey portrayed in movies and plays time and time again. But never had I noticed a true-to-text depiction of what the prophecy of Zechariah 9:9 declares, and what Matthew 21 reveals, until recently. Jesus didn't just ride on a donkey; He rode on a donkey and a colt. We see a perfect picture of the concept of leadership bestowed upon a mother. This was a joint calling and a joint destiny. It was a mother donkey that Jesus sent for, and her little baby colt was with her. Jesus did not just call for one. He called for *both* of them. Their destiny was intertwined. One was not in the way of the other because both were necessary for fulfillment.

In this case the mother was likely owned by someone for work or travel purposes and was tied up daily. The colt was born into the bondage of his mother, owned from birth by the same master. The colt never knew the concept of freedom. Even though both the mother and the colt could have been tied up, I have often wondered if a rope was even needed for the colt. Because of his attachment to his mother and the limits of her own mobility, wouldn't the colt have adopted her bondage with or without a rope? Because this colt saw the model of bondage every day from its mother, his rope could have been mental rather than just literal. It was emotional and part of his inheritance. Rather than a positive inheritance, as we normally think of, this was inherited bondage. The colt nursed by the rope, slept by the rope, and lived by the rope of his mother for so long that it became his own rope. It was the only reality he knew.

Our children will follow us wherever we lead them, whether it is into the freedom of Christ or the bondage of the enemy.

Without the disciples performing the act of loosing the mother, the child never would have become free. I am convinced that even if the colt had been loosed but the mother had not been, the colt would have remained with her as she remained in bondage. This is the concept of motherly leadership. Our children will follow us wherever we lead them, whether it is into the freedom of Christ or the bondage of the enemy. Whether it is into the destiny they were created for or the prison the enemy designed for them, the calling of God the Father envelops both the mother and the child; the two are difficult to separate. Where are you leading your child, Mom? And what rope are you teaching her to adopt as her own? It took the loosing and leading of the mother to also bring the freedom and destiny of the colt.

WHAT IS YOUR "ROPE"?

I sat in a class of mothers one evening and asked this question: "What is your rope? What is that thing in your life that keeps you close to the post and keeps you from following the call of God? What is it that pulls you back every time you try to move forward to Christ?" Tears flowed down every cheek as all began to recognize the bondage that they had carried for far too long. Fear, insecurity, addictions, abuse, and anxiety were all ropes that were identified that night. We are sometimes satisfied just to manage bondage or try to ignore it and hope no one else sees our ropes. We so often are satisfied to live in our own compromise, and we refuse to take the time to focus on our own needs until we look down by our side one day and realize our children are adopting our bondage, our mind-sets, our fears, our insecurities, and our addictions. They are following us to the same confinement we were taught. The enemy doesn't even have to work hard to capture our children; we do the work for him by modeling our own ropes before them. We model bondage, and therefore they follow bondage.

Don't be disheartened. In this story we see hope! That hope is Christ, and His voice is calling for us. When He has need of you, no rope and no taskmaster can stand in the way! It didn't matter how many days or years that mother and baby donkey had lived in bondage; Jesus saw them that day and had need of them. This fact shifted everything. He sent for them and gave the authority to His disciples to loose them and bring them to the place of destiny. Similarly Jesus needs you and your babies! The post you are tied to is not your final destination, and the enemy is no longer your master. I stand in the authority of Jesus Christ today, woman of God, and I declare that every rope over your life be removed in Jesus's name! He needs you. The kingdom needs you. You were called to a greater purpose than to be the slave to the enemy, and your child has a greater purpose than to repeat the cycles that have held you bound. He is calling for both of you, and it is time to sever the rope once and for all. It's time to lead your child to Him.

When the mother was loosed, she had to be willing to be led, but not by her former master; she had to be willing to be led by those who were following the voice of Christ. She was led to Him, and her child followed. For the first time the son or daughter saw the mother under new leadership and without the post. This was a new path they were walking, and it would lead to a new future. The mother pursued Christ, and the baby was set up for a divine appointment and prophetic fulfillment. When the mother found freedom, the baby found destiny. The mother's ceiling became her child's floor, and that colt became the vehicle of the Messiah for all of Jerusalem to see. The donkey and the colt were both selected in bondage to be set free for a great purpose that was written before either of them were born. The Word found them, the Word freed them, and the Word will never return void, not in this story and not in your story (Isa. 55:11).

You don't have to stay confined to that post one day longer, Mom. Right now you can be free. You can begin a new story for your children and your grandchildren to inherit freedom and not slavery, to follow the path of life and not bondage to sin. You have been loosed so that you can lead.

> I declare this freedom over you today, and I sever every rope of the enemy in Jesus's name. I declare every generational rope that you have learned will not be passed to your children. I declare the cycles that have held you bound stop today, as truth brings freedom. I declare a new journey starts for you and your seed, a path that fulfills kingdom promise and prophetic destiny. The Lord is calling because He has need of you, and by His Word I loose you to run after Him! ❖

Chapter Four
KEEPING YOUR CHILDREN ON COURSE

THIS PAST SCHOOL year I received one of those calls that every mother dreads to receive. Since I am the mother of two teenagers, it is not uncommon for the school number to show up on my phone. Whether it is a forgotten lunch or missing gym clothes, I am accustomed to hearing from my boys during their school day. However, when I saw the school's number and answered the phone, I was caught off guard by the voice of one of the staff members on the line. "Mrs. Wallace," the lady said, "we have been trying to reach you, and we need you to come to the school immediately." My heart dropped, and by the tone in her voice I was afraid to ask questions. She said, "It's your son, Jeremiah. He has hurt his arm and will need to be taken to the ER." A strange sense of relief swept over me that at least it wasn't worse. "Do you think it is broken?" I asked, and she said, "His wrist is broken; that we know for sure."

Normally I am within five minutes of my kids' school at all times because of the location of our home and church, but on this day I was more than twenty minutes away. I sped like a wild woman, and my imagination was running wild. It wasn't even lunchtime yet, so how in the world could he have broken his arm? He should have only been in class by that point. "Is he conscious? Is he crying in front of his friends? Is he scared? Why am I not closer?" These questions endlessly ran through my mind as I prayed and raced to his rescue.

When I arrived, I saw the principal himself sitting with my son in the sick room with one of the athletic trainers, and I knew it had to be bad. They had placed a temporary splint on Jeremiah's arm because the bone was pressing against his skin and the arm was so contorted.

I didn't have words. I just showed them to my car and asked Jeremiah if he was OK. He was silent, and his face was pale, and as soon as they shut my car door and we began to pull away from the school, my strong boy just melted into a puddle of tears. "Mom, it hurts," he cried. He had held his emotions in until he finally felt safe in the car with me. "I don't understand," he cried. "I was just doing something I have done before. I jumped up to touch the ceiling of the hallway on my way to class, and it was like someone just knocked my feet out from under me! I promise that's what it felt like, Mom!"

I wondered if someone really did do that, but the witnesses on the scene and even the security video showed that no one touched my little man. Yet somehow his feet came up and completely out from under him in the short hop that he had indeed taken many times before. I could not wrap my mind around it as we drove. Every bump in the road led to another cry of pain until we finally reached the ER.

It was broken; his arm had snapped in two midway between the wrist and elbow. It was a serious break that would require many x-rays and visits to the doctor, and even multiple casts. It wasn't until a day after the incident, when the shock wore off, that we realized the true impact of that moment. That one moment would change the course of the rest of Jeremiah's life. It was a pivotal moment that God, in His mercy, had allowed. It was one of those answers to a prayer that you wouldn't pray if you really understood the actions it would take to achieve such an answer. It was the beginning of a journey that again transitioned the way I parented and the way I understood how God's hand shapes my children's destinies. It humbled me as a mother and instructed me at the same time.

RESTORING BROKEN DESTINY

Jeremiah was and still is a natural-born athlete. It seems to be woven in his DNA. I have fond memories of him playing T-ball at three and never using the tee. I remember celebrating touchdowns and cheering after three-pointers. I celebrated golf games where he came under par, and I even remember him taking a shot at swim team for a semester. He loved all sports and seemed to have the ability to hold his own in any sport he tried. He lived to be active, and our schedule reflected

God is more concerned with your character than your comfort.

that. At the time of his injury he was approaching a state tournament for golf and had just started a new AAU basketball team. Decisions concerning summer training for football were right around the corner, and all of the above were setting the pace for his high school career. That one moment brought everything in his little world to a screeching halt. All of his sport obligations suddenly took a backseat to his current physical condition. No human hands could control it or change it. Even his ability to be active at home changed; we had just built a new pool, and the kids had patiently waited on its completion. Jeremiah missed out on the joys of summer fun at home, and we had to delay vacation plans and rework life in general.

He was brokenhearted, and so were Kevin and I. I found

myself doing what any Pentecostal Christian would do: I started rebuking the devil and praying for healing. It was during my intense time of crying out for life to return to normal for Jeremiah that the Lord wrecked my prayers. God said, "I am resetting him."

"What? You mean somehow You are in this?" I responded.

Yes, I know this is theologically challenging for some, but it was as if the Holy Spirit let me know He was in control in this. He assured me that He would give grace, but that healing would come over time. God was doing something bigger behind the scenes. The arm was not the Lord's concern, but Jeremiah's future was of greater weight in this circumstance.

In that moment I remembered a saying from a pastor I once heard: God is more concerned with your character than your comfort. It's hard for us to imagine God would ever allow something painful or negative to happen to us, but He doesn't sit in heaven and try to think of ways to make us more comfortable in life. He is continually working on our behalf to get us to His divine purpose and destiny. Sometimes comfort is the enemy of that. Sometimes comfort is our enemy and the enemy of our children, and pain can be our best friend and teacher. It became clear that this was somehow a divine interruption and a time when the Lord was using what the enemy meant for evil for Jeremiah's good.

BENCHED FOR A SEASON

No one likes pain. What is even more difficult for me than experiencing pain myself is watching my children experience pain. As a mother it is my instinct to do everything in my power to stop it! However, pain can be a friend, and it most certainly is a gift from God.

Don't believe me? Look at the sensation of pain itself. It

is a negative experience yet a God-ordained feeling. It isn't pleasant, but it is necessary. It is the body's way of preserving itself. Pain is meant to stop our dangerous actions or warn us of danger within our bodies. Without the presence of the negative feeling of pain, we could cut off a finger or bleed to death from a cut without even realizing it. We could become sick and get to the point of death and be clueless that something is even wrong. We could set a hand on a hot stove, causing our skin to blister but never realizing we should move our hand if we did not have the sensation of pain to warn us.

Pain shapes us and shapes our perspective of life.

This is why discipline is coupled with pain and discomfort. It challenges us to move away from dangerous behavior, even if we desire it. God is the righteous parent that at times allows pain in our lives to keep us from harming ourselves not only in the natural but also in the spirit. Pain is sometimes meant to scream that we are headed in the wrong direction and divert us from killing our destinies. Discipline without some form of pain or discomfort is not effective. There must be an association between negative actions equaling negative results.

I was grieving over a broken arm, but God was grieving over a broken destiny. I was worried about Jeremiah's current comfort and his current sports schedule, but God was concerned for his future. The broken arm was not God's focal point; it was a prophetic sign of a bigger issue. At first I was so busy focusing on the minor issue that I almost missed the major one. When God said He was resetting Jeremiah, I realized that in the madness of life I had allowed my son to begin to venture off course. God was looking at something bigger and was calling a clear "time-out" in Jeremiah's life—a complete and total time-out that benched him for the season. This break wasn't just a fracture he could continue to function with or push through; it was severe and complete and required him to be completely still. Jeremiah was in need of a life reset.

According to Merriam-Webster, to *reset* something means to move it "back to its original place or position."[1] If Jeremiah needed to be reset, it meant he obviously was out of place or position. But how did we get there? How did I as a praying, prophesying, book-writing mother allow my son to get out of position? Even worse, how did I lead him there?

God said to me, "Deven, don't mold Jeremiah in ways that I have to break him from." Jeremiah's arm was out of whack as much as his life was, and I shared in the responsibility of creating that. I could not reset his life any more than I could reset his broken arm. I needed professional help. Only a doctor could help his arm heal back in the intended position, and only God could reset his intended destiny.

Getting off course and needing a reset doesn't always just happen overnight or in a single moment. If getting out of position was that obvious, every praying mother would see it immediately. Many times getting off course is something that happens over time. A dear friend once told me that every degree on a compass matters. If a ship sets sail and is just one degree off at the onset of its journey, that one degree will equal miles by the end of the journey. The direction our children take and the choices they make in their early years may not seem significant at the time, but their future is greatly affected by their choices. We cannot afford to miss the small degrees at the beginning, when we are shaping the arrows that God has entrusted to us. Even daily decisions that seem insignificant could be mile-producing degrees over time.

This was the scenario in our family. We had taken a course that set us just a few degrees off in the beginning, but as Jeremiah began to mature and grow into adulthood, it began to lead him further and further from his intended target. It was a carefully crafted plan of diversion that took place over a chunk of time. Little by little, inch by inch, we began to walk with Jeremiah down a pathway that was not part of his destined future, a pathway that would have actually taken him not only off course but also in the opposite direction. However, because we pray and seek God regularly over our children for their destinies and their futures, God in His mercy allowed a little temporary discomfort to realign Jeremiah for his intended future. God in His mercy intervened even when I as a parent was part of the problem.

I declare alignment over our homes, Lord Jesus. We pray You will gently reveal anything we prioritize that is not in line with Your purpose over our families. I declare that our eyes would be opened as mothers to motives and passions in our hearts that could become obstacles or hindrances to our children's destinies in You. In the mercy of Your divine intervention, realign us with Your heart and Your will, Father. We give you permission to reset our homes where needed and refocus our priorities. ❖

Chapter Five
RAISING "LEFT-HANDED" WARRIORS

>>>———————————————>

DURING THE SAME time frame as Jeremiah's broken arm incident, I was also preparing for our annual moms conference at our church. This is a gathering very dear to my heart with two power-packed days set aside for mothers to be equipped and to have the opportunity to encounter God without distraction or interruption. As I was praying and fasting for God to download into my heart His word and agenda for the gathering, He began to deal with me about a very familiar story found in Judges 3 of a judge and deliverer of Israel known as Ehud. My son just happened to be currently reading through the Book of Judges and was also captured by this unusual and slightly graphic story. What boy wouldn't be? Ehud was an unassuming warrior who became a necessary instrument for the victory of Israel.

Ehud was sent to meet face-to-face with the wicked King Eglon under the disguise of being the chosen deliverer of a gift. The real agenda was the destruction of the king. But how? Why was this young man chosen, and how did he get face-to-face with the wicked ruler? It was because he had a secret skill that many may have considered a handicap. He had a particular ability that allowed him to slip past security with his weapon of choice. Ehud was left-handed (Judg. 3:15). It was not normal for warriors to be left-handed, so the king's security only checked Ehud's left thigh for a weapon, assuming he was a right-handed man. In order to draw a sword, he would have been trained to reach across his body to the opposite side. Because he could use a weapon from the right side, his dagger would go undetected by the foolish assumption of the enemy. That is why he was chosen to deliver a present to King Eglon.

WHEN WEAKNESS BECOMES STRENGTH

Isn't it just like God to take what others would consider a setback and use it as a setup in the kingdom? The thought began to stir in my heart about how our children are sometimes viewed and labeled. When placed against a canvas of what we deem normal, many mothers find that their children are being labeled with handicaps and setbacks that seem to separate them from "success." Our God, however, is the God of the underdog. It has been and will continue to be His pattern and nature to use "the foolish things of the world to confound the wise," according to 1 Corinthians 1:27. He sees what the world deems weakness and forges it as a strength. God's glory is not known in the abilities of a man or woman's strength, but in His ability through their weaknesses. In fact, the Word says in 2 Chronicles 16:9 that God is searching for the weak to show Himself strong on their behalf. As hard as it is for our minds to comprehend, sometimes great strengths can disqualify us from His glory, and great weaknesses can often be the choice platform of the Lord. Look at Gideon's army in Judges 7. It was the unassuming, underestimated army that God chose to use to win the victory. And He only wanted a remnant of three hundred! Similarly God chose what would be considered the weaker warrior with the story of Ehud; he was left-handed, but God anointed him for battle!

There is a deeper layer behind the deliverer known as

Ehud—one that enlightens us to understand why he was ready for this assignment. The truth is that Ehud had been trained for it his entire life. He was trained to be left-handed! He was chosen to obtain a skill with his weak side in order to give his tribe a military advantage. He was of the tribe of Benjamin. This tribe understood the value of surprising the enemy, and those in it embraced the true strength that rested on the weak and unsuspecting side, the left side. History tells us that the tribe of Benjamin chose seven hundred warriors to be slingers in battle with the left hand (Judg. 20:16). Many today have argued how this came to be. Could they have been born left-handed, or were they warriors who had been wounded on the right side so they trained themselves on the left side? First Chronicles 12:2 gives us an even deeper clue about this tribe, stating that its members were ambidextrous. They had use of their right hand as well as their left. Were they born this way, or were they born right-handed and made to use their left hand, therefore gaining the ability to use both?

The Benjamites may have been born right-handed but forced to use their left hand, and the core of the evidence for this concept is seen in the word used for "left-handed" in the original text. The Hebrew reading of this passage concerning Ehud and the other seven hundred left-handed warriors actually reads as bound or restricted in the right hand.[1] It doesn't actually refer to the left hand at all. These particular chosen warriors were actually trained to use the left hand so skillfully because they were bound up or tied up on their right side. These restrictions forced a change in operation for them. They were trained to lean upon their weak side until it became their strength. This unique strategy gave them a military advantage that made them a lethal weapon in battle.

Common sense would lead us to conclude that this left-handed training could not begin on the first day of hand-to-hand combat. It had to be an intentional reshaping of a young man's, even a boy's, fine and gross motor skills. These seven hundred warriors actually were training the brain to operate from the opposite side! It is the right side of the brain that controls the left side of the body, and vice versa. Therefore training to use the left side would be strengthening the efforts of the right side of the brain. This training would need to begin during the formative stages of the child's operation development to make the transition easier and more successful. This would be during the preschool and early primary grades, as most educators and mothers know. That changes everything! It actually reveals a Jedi-type model of battle training! It means the tribe of Benjamin probably chose young boys and restricted them in their right hand in order to force dominance on their left side.

GOD'S INGENIOUS BATTLE STRATEGY

My mother once told me that when she was in elementary school it was considered negative to be left-handed. Obviously at that point our society did not know how to accept the uniqueness of a child. She remembered when teachers forced the left-handed children to use their right hands during daily classroom activities and during handwriting in order to change them from being left-handed to being right-handed. This was still the case when my older brother attended school. His teacher required him, a left-handed kindergartner, to use his right hand, and eventually he gained the necessary strength to write correctly with it. To this day he is still ambidextrous. He never lost the use of his born tendency to use the left hand, but he did gain the skill and strength to write with his right hand. Educators knew that this skill set had to be developed early in life and had to be taught through daily consistent exercises if they were going to achieve their goal. I believe the Benjamites knew that also! I believe the left-handed warriors of the tribe of Benjamin were trained as young children, and many scholars believe this theory as well.

The restriction by binding of the right hand had to start when these men were children in order to be effective, and it had to be woven into everyday life. Before the father or soldier ever taught a child to sling a rock with his left hand, somewhere his mother made him eat his breakfast before school with his left hand. Before he ever swung a sword at a target using the left hand, his mother bound his right hand as he played with his friends. It was the mothers, I believe, who participated in the daily restriction of the right hands of their chosen sons so that the left hands could become lethal weapons. It was seemingly excessive and somewhat strange parenting that actually proved to be an ingenious battle strategy. Although they may have been criticized, their efforts soon benefited the whole tribe!

When I think of "left-handed" mothers, those who didn't conform their parenting to the norms of society in order to do what the Holy Spirit was leading them to do for their children, I think of Jochebed, Moses's mother. She rescued her nation by daring to release her son to unusual circumstances at an early age. I think of Elizabeth, who had to let her little boy hang out in the wilderness and eat strange foods in order to aid in the deliverance of Israel. I think of Hannah, who released Samuel to his training in the temple in his pre-school years. It was these mothers walking in obedience to unusual and excessive tactics at such an early age that proved to create lethal weapons against the enemy! These mothers were given arrows, and they shaped them for impact!

SONS AND DAUGHTERS OF HIS RIGHT HAND

How ironic is it that the name *Benjamin* means "son of my right hand"?[2] What? The tribe named "son of my right hand" was chosen to be left-handed? This was something I had to take to the Lord in prayer in order to gain clarity. To be a son of the right hand in the natural meant to be right-handed and to operate with strength from the left side of the brain. The left side of the brain also controls human reasoning and intellect. To become left-handed would mean to strengthen the right side of the brain. The right side of the brain controls creativity and our "artsy" side. It is with the left side of our brain that we process information and develop logical thoughts and solutions, while it is with the right side of the brain that we sense, feel, experience emotions, and even experience God. Left side is logic, and right side is creativity, and each side of the brain controls the opposite side of the body. To be right-handed could spiritually symbolize leaning on logic and human reasoning, while to be left-handed could symbolize finding strength in the creative, emotional, and experiential side of the brain. Switching from spiritual left-brain operation to spiritual right-brain operation would move us from our own reasoning and understanding to a God-centered perspective of life. It reminds me of a familiar passage in Proverbs 3:5 that warns us to, "Trust in the LORD with all your heart, and lean not on your own understanding." Transitioning from right-hand operation to left-hand operation is then a true shift in thinking and a renewing of the mind.

Culturally and spiritually to the Hebrew people, to be a son of the right hand meant that you were positioned in strength and were marked for blessing. In the Bible the father would use his right hand to pass the blessing on to his children. It was the hand of favor and blessing. If the left hand was used, it was an inferior blessing, as seen in Genesis 48 when Jacob crossed his hands to bestow the right-handed blessing upon his younger son instead of the elder son as was customary. It was necessary for his right hand to be laid upon the head of the younger son for the transaction to take place. That right hand was one of fatherly authority. The son of the right hand was favored by the father and would receive a greater inheritance.

The right hand also demonstrates the strength of God. Exodus 15:6 reads, "Your right hand, O LORD, is glorious in power. Your right hand, O LORD, shatters the enemy." Psalm 89:13 states, "You have a mighty arm, and strong is Your hand, and victorious is Your right hand." And there are more than fifty other scriptures that speak of the right hand of God. It is His right hand that represents His power to deliver and power to save. It is His fatherly right hand that represents His power to bless and multiply His sons and daughters.

In seeking God, I had to ask, "Lord, how can You call the tribe of Benjamin sons of Your right hand, yet those tribe members be characterized by restricting their right hands to utilize their left? Can left-handed warriors be sons of Your right hand? Everything about the left hand seems weak and inferior." God said, "If you are going to be a son or daughter of My right hand (blessing, favor, strength, and authority), then you cannot be a son or daughter of your right hand. Those who will be sons and daughters of My strength must not lean on their own strength." In other words, if you are going to experience God's strength, you must operate in your weakness. If you are going to be of His right hand, your right hand cannot get in the way. It was by design that He called the left-handed warriors "sons of His right hand." They were dependent upon Him.

This is not about being physically right-handed or left-handed. This is a deeper revelation about being more right-handed or left-handed in the Spirit. It is a physical representation of a deeper spiritual truth. It is in your weakness that His strength is made perfect (2 Cor. 12:9). Leaning on your left hand can perfect the right hand of God in your life. Those who walk in God's blessing and favor must not depend on their own ability to achieve blessing or on any earthly father's ability to bless and favor them. Just look at Jacob, who still had to wrestle God for the real blessing even though his earthly father blessed him. The earthly blessing was temporal and incomplete, and Jacob had achieved it in his own strength, which is in essence him leaning on his own right hand. Earthly favor gained by fleshly means will fall short, but heavenly favor is irrevocable. Jacob looked to the right hand of his earthly father, but he needed the right hand of his heavenly Father.

If you are going to experience God's strength, you must operate in your weakness. If you are going to be of His right hand, your right hand cannot get in the way.

God would not put His right hand of blessing on him until Jacob was humbled before Him. God dislocated his hip so he could no longer lean on his own strength (Gen. 32:25). Although Scripture does not clearly articulate which hip God touched, I would like to imagine it was his right hip. Jacob became a son of God's right hand when he began to operate by his left hand in the Spirit.

Those who are of God's right hand must not lean on their own intellect and reasoning, but they must hear and obey the voice of God and God alone. Spiritually a right-handed individual would represent the left-brain thinking of logic and reason, yet the Word lets us know our intellect and wisdom are far inferior to the mind of God. This is why the Word says in Proverbs 3:5 that we should "trust in the LORD with all your heart, and lean not on your own understanding." It was human reasoning that led Adam and Eve to sin in the beginning when Eve took the fruit. She bought the logic of the enemy. It is human reasoning that will hinder a son's or daughter's ability to walk in radical obedience to God. Human wisdom is foolishness to God (1 Cor. 3:19), and His ways are radically higher than human ways (Isa. 55:8–9). We must train our children to follow God's leading over their own reasoning, walking by wisdom that comes from the heavenly realm and not from the earthly realm.

Through this revelation God literally rocked my world; my thinking on how I was shaping and training my own son changed. It was in the middle of studying this word from the Lord that Jeremiah broke his arm, and it was Jeremiah's right arm that was broken! Ironically it wasn't until midway through my actually preaching this word at the moms conference that the Holy Spirit removed the veil from my eyes and enlightened me. God was not just downloading revelation to me for mothers of this generation. He was downloading to me understanding about this difficult season in Jeremiah's life! God was resetting Jeremiah to be a left-handed warrior, not a right-handed one! I had been training Jeremiah to lean on his own strength and abilities. I was teaching him to

lean on his own gifts and desires. Even though the phenom-
enal school he was enrolled in was giving him a great education, it was training him to walk in human reasoning and
wisdom and teaching him the world's standards of success
for his future. God was letting me know that I was molding
Jeremiah with a mind-set and philosophy of life that God
would have to break in him later if it wasn't broken in him
now! The whole scenario of this painful journey was a tremendous act of grace. God was teaching me that if I wanted
my children, and at that time my eldest son, Jeremiah, to be
a son of God's right hand, he could not rely on his own right
hand. It was a physical break that God used to demonstrate
a spiritual truth.

God solidified this revelation by showing me the illustra-
tion of me walking down the sidewalk with my son, hand in
hand. In order for me to have Jeremiah by my right hand, my
hand of strength, I had to walk holding his left hand, repre-
senting his hand of weakness. If I tried to walk holding his
right hand in my right hand, it would have been an awkward obstacle for us to walk in harmony together. God let
me know that day that if Jeremiah was going to walk hand
in hand with the Lord, a hand switch had to take place! God
wanted Jeremiah's left hand to take His right so the Lord
could show Himself mighty in Jeremiah's life and receive all
the glory!

RESET FROM THE INSIDE OUT

Kevin and I repented before the Lord and asked for His
help in resetting Jeremiah's life, and this situation just happened to take place at the onset of high school. We were so
thankful God allowed this to happen at this strategic junc-
ture in Jeremiah's early development instead of later in life.

As with any break, the longer it stays out of place before being reset, the more difficult it is to heal. It was as if God in His grace allowed for the reset to happen early.

I reflected on my own life and how the Lord had to radically change my perspective as a young college student. I was heading full force down a pathway that satisfied my desires and was fueled by my own gifts and abilities. I was asking God to bless my plans when He had better ones for me. It took a breaking season for me to see that, and I often look back and think about all the time I invested in a life path that would have never fulfilled me! God had placed a call of ministry in my life, but my strong logic and reasoning skills could not understand it. I wanted to be a doctor, but God had called me to be a preacher. It was a painful but necessary season of resetting, and I thank God for every moment of it. I cannot imagine what my life would be like today if I had not allowed God to reset me from the inside out! Now in His grace and mercy He was intervening on behalf of my son!

Kevin and I were ready and willing to obey His divine instruction. God was faithful to begin to communicate with Jeremiah also. His downtime gave him the ability to hear God and see the need for change. God began to remold his desires, and Kevin and I joyfully watched Jeremiah make some incredible yet difficult decisions on his own. We stood back and allowed God to reshape and remold our son. In the physical, as Jeremiah wore his cast, I watched my son begin to do things with his left hand that he could normally achieve only with his right. In the natural he was gaining strength on his weak side because he was bound on the right side! I knew the same thing was happening in the Spirit. Jeremiah's spirit man was growing stronger, and he began to strengthen parts of his life that were weak and neglected.

His life had been restricted in many aspects in his normal strengths and desires, but it only increased strength in the more important areas. His daily life was changing, and his life focus was aligning with God's heart for him.

That summer we took some of the most radical and strategic leaps of faith with our children we had ever taken. Many of the decisions we made seemed to "come out of left field," as the old saying goes. That is exactly what happened; they came from the left side. We made those types of decisions that drive a mother to fast and experience many sleepless nights of prayer. For the first time we really began to let Jeremiah steer some major decisions over his life (within reason, of course), while his father and I prayed and guided him. I felt we were in a wrestling match with Jeremiah's destiny, and we had to hear the Spirit of the Lord for what to do next. Every decision seemed to matter, and God was making Himself very clear.

Jeremiah's focus changed first, and then his schedule followed. We had to start organizing his life around God-given desires and goals rather than around cultural expectations or selfish ambition. God had to be the priority and central driving force every day of Jeremiah's life. The Lord was refusing to become a side dish to Jeremiah's future. Jeremiah's educational plan changed in every way, including his school. His sports schedule was simplified, and even his friendships began to shift. The daily atmosphere of his life was changing, and it was leading change for all of our children. God let me know that atmosphere and climate were vital to the successful growth of all my babies. Good seed in the wrong climate can fail to produce. They all had to be placed in an environment for maximum growth. The kingdom was within them; they must be in the right climate for fruit to produce.

Looking back now, I thank God for the summer Jeremiah broke his arm. I never saw it coming and would have tried everything to prevent it had I known. But now it is slightly terrifying for me to think of where Jeremiah would be if God had not allowed this season of intervention. I had to become the trainer of a left-handed warrior and realize that my parenting style and decisions may not fit in with what is the cultural norm or latest trend. But in the end this type of parenting would produce an arrow of great impact.

God desires for our children to be left-handed in the Spirit, no longer leaning on their own strength or understanding, but His. He is crafting those who take the enemy by surprise by not operating on their own strong side, but the Lord's. He is searching for mothers who can train such warriors, mothers who aren't afraid to adopt spiritually left-handed thinking and left-handed parenting styles. We as kingdom-minded mothers cannot always look to society to understand how to shape our arrows. God's ways will not always make sense. We must lean on the wisdom and instruction of God even in the early stages of our children's growth and development. We must train them to lean on Him and operate in their unique skill sets!

Everyone wasn't trained to be left-handed because only a few were needed. That small remnant, however, won many battles for their entire tribe. God didn't need everyone to accomplish His purpose. He just needed someone who would obey.

I declare in the name of Jesus that a remnant of left-handed-thinking mothers would rise to their calling so we can see a whole army of skilled warriors take the kingdom of darkness by surprise. The enemy thinks he has this generation figured out, but I declare God is raising up His own army that will confuse the powers of darkness with unique strategy and anointing. In the name of Jesus may a group of radical, sold-out, Spirit-filled, and obedient young people rise up. This will not fit in with popular culture, but it can quite possibly bring victory for our entire nation and the nations of the earth. May those in this generation shift their thinking from human limitations, and may the Lord anoint young men and women intentionally restricted on their right hands in order to be guided by His right hand, leading their peers from the left side! ❖

Chapter Six
RESTORING THE WAYWARD CHILD

>>>+-----------------+

IN 1 KINGS 3 WE find a very familiar story that is purposed to display the magnitude of the wisdom that God had gifted to Solomon. However, if we look at this story together a little more closely, we will find a deeper message that I believe speaks to mothers, particularly mothers whose children have been deceived or ensnared by the enemy.

Two prostitutes came before the king with a dilemma. They lived in the same house and participated in the same sinful lifestyle, and both of them just happened to have given birth to baby boys just a few days apart. Both of the women shared the same experience of birth, but they had two very different responses to motherhood. A prostitute under normal circumstances would never attempt to get pregnant on the job. The pregnancy alone would simply hinder her ability to work and earn an income. (I know this all too well from my work with survivors of human trafficking.) It is likely that neither of these women sought out motherhood, and both could have been saddened or disappointed by the initial news. Something shifted, however, over one of the mothers from the moment she held her baby boy in her arms. Something shifted in her heart to have love and compassion for her child. In just a few moments a woman who had lived a sinful life of promiscuity was overcome with the heart and love of a mother.

The other prostitute, however, seemed more concerned

with the concept of motherhood than the son who gave her the title of mother. She lacked compassion and selfless love. It was a competition to her; it was not about the well-being of either her child or the other woman's son. It was about a title and not about a child. One night both of these women fell asleep with their babies at their sides.

So much could be said about the risk of a baby beside a sleeping mother. In the natural we know this is a huge health risk. In this moment, however, I am not talking about the natural risk, although it is obvious. There is a spiritual layer here that I don't want you to miss. Although we as mothers rarely get to sleep in the natural, it is necessary that we do sleep a certain number of hours per day in order to function. In the spirit, however, we are never to fall asleep while our children lie at our sides. Our spirits are not created to sleep, only to rest. God Himself does not sleep, according to Psalm 121:4, but He does rest, as we see in the Creation story (Gen. 2:2–3). Your spirit has to learn to move from warfare to rest, but it must never be allowed to drift off to sleep.

AWAKE IN THE BODY, ASLEEP IN THE SPIRIT

We can see the difference in rest and sleep in Matthew 8, as Christ was sailing with His disciples from one side of the Sea of Galilee to the other. A storm arose, and the disciples were awake and frantically fighting the storm while Jesus was asleep in the bottom of the boat. His body had drifted off to sleep, but the story lets us know His spirit was wide awake. As soon as they stirred His body, His spirit spoke with authority against the storm, and the sea obeyed (vv. 24–26). He was "ready in season and out of season" and walked in authority because His spirit was alert and connected with God (2 Tim. 4:2).

The disciples were awake in their bodies but asleep in the spirit. Even though their eyes were open during the storm, their spirits were dormant in the ability to walk in authority over the storm. They rowed, and they worked, but they did not accomplish anything. Jesus was asleep in the natural but awake in the Spirit. He accomplished more from a place of rest than they did in all their worry and turmoil. The most effective way we can war for our children is to do so from a place of spiritual alertness, even while we are sleeping, and from a place of rest in God's Word rather than a place of worry and anxiety. It is that kind of faith, even in a storm, that moves the hand of God.

> **Not only is spiritual slumber dangerous to you as a mother, but it also puts your children at risk.**

I fear for this generation because I fear that there are too many sleeping mothers who have put their young ones at risk, mothers participating in reckless spiritual behavior and apathy that endanger the lives and breath of their children. These mothers may be awake in the natural, and even really busy with motherly activities, but they are unaware in their spirit, walking without authority or insight in the spirit realm. They are worrying and working, leaning on their own strength instead of leaning on Him. They are rowing but not making any progress. No mother in her right mind would willingly roll over onto her child and suffocate the baby. However, when a mother is asleep, she is unaware and numb to the impact of her own actions and the damage it is causing to her child. Not only is spiritual slumber dangerous to you as a mother, but it also puts your children at risk.

The truth is the lifestyle of the mother written about in 1 Kings 3 placed her child in an atmosphere of danger and uncertainty, taking the breath and life of her baby. I think we as mothers have all experienced this to an extent. We have lived lifestyles or made choices for which our children end up suffering. You may be a mother who did not raise your children in a godly home with godly standards. Maybe you didn't even find Jesus yourself until later in life. Maybe you live every day with regret for allowing your own issues to harm the futures of your children. Or maybe you have just lived the life of a sleeping mom, raising your children with no sensitivity to or awareness of the enemy or the Spirit of God. Now you find yourself holding a dead baby, a child who once lived but is now void of breath.

The story tells us that after the first mother suffocated her child in her slumber, she decided to sneak over to the bedside of her friend and snatch her little boy while that mother also slept. The first mother literally switched out her roommate's live baby and replaced him with her dead son (1 Kings 3:19–20). Now that is some deep sleep! The mother of the live son did not even awaken as her enemy stole what was precious to her. She didn't even stir. Not only does a sleeping mother run the risk of harming her own child, but a sleeping mother is also unaware of the presence of her enemy. When a mother is asleep in the spirit, the devil can walk right up to her house, right up to her child, and take what doesn't belong to him. This has been the plan of the enemy all along: he wants to take what doesn't belong to him because he cannot produce life or dominion himself. He can only steal the lives and dominion of the children of God. The wicked mother took the living child as her own and left a dead baby lying in the arms of the sleeping mother.

THE POWER OF A MOTHER'S AWAKENING

As the mother opened her eyes in the dark, she had limited perspective because she was still partially asleep. Her perception was not clear as long as she drifted in and out of slumber. In her limited vision she thought the dead child was her own. She could not see clearly. She could only see what her enemy wanted her to see—the dead baby. She bought the lie the enemy planned for her, and she thought her child was dead.

That being said, as morning came, the light began to shine, and the mother finally woke up, and her eyes could see beyond the deception she had been set up for. This is the power of a mother's awakening. When we wake up, we can see truth, even if it's ugly. When we wake up, we can shake ourselves from the deception the enemy has planted in our hearts and homes. When a mother wakes up, she can see what no one else can see, for she knows the truth of her child's identity. In the morning light this particular mother realized immediately that this dead baby was not her child! The devil may deceive a friend, grandparent, or teacher, but the devil cannot deceive a mother who is awake and alert. She is like a fierce lioness that will defend what has been entrusted to her.

Light awakens. Light exposes deception and illuminates truth, setting us free from bondage. I pray that even now the truth of God's Word would be like the morning sun over you, Mom, and it would awaken you from apathy and deception. Wake up as this mother did and declare, "That's not my child!" I don't care how dead your son or daughter may seem in the spirit. I don't care how far he or she has strayed from the Lord. I don't care if you were asleep and unable to stop the plan of the enemy. It doesn't matter if it's drugs, promiscuity, hard-heartedness, or rebellion. Don't you buy the lie of the enemy over your baby! That dead child in your arms and in your home is not your child! That is the enemy's version of your baby, and he wants you to settle for his plan. Lift your voice in defiance of the lie, and take that dead baby straight to the King. He is the only One who can expose your enemy and restore your true child back to your arms.

That's exactly what this mother did. She did not remain silent and apathetic. She was awake and dangerous, and she would not be denied justice. Without hesitation she lifted her case to the highest authority, the king (1 Kings 3:16). You are an advocate, Mom! In a season that the enemy has deceived you and your child seems to be right in the cradle of his arms, whether it's by your child's own choice or by your mistakes, you cannot remain silent. No longer will you sleep, but now you must lift your voice as an advocate to heaven on your child's behalf. Refuse to be denied what rightfully belongs to you, and do not relent until you have what does not belong in the arms of the enemy. Like the little widow in Luke 18, who wearied the judge with her persistence, don't stop until heaven hears and answers. Tell the devil, and tell the King, "That's not my child!" Declare, "My child will live and not die and declare the works of the Lord!" (Ps. 118:17).

In the story, as the prostitutes began fighting over the one living child, the king heard the cry of the mother and in his wisdom set up a plan to expose the foothold of the enemy. He designed a situation that would cause the enemy's plan to backfire. What he designed to do seemed as if it agreed with what the wicked mother wanted and fed into the plans of the enemy. What the king did seemed to be purposed to destroy what life was left in the son. In fact, his decree seemed as if it was a setup for destruction (1 Kings 3:24–25). Sometimes God answers our prayers in ways we don't expect or understand.

Isaiah 55:8–9 tells us that His ways are not our ways and His thoughts are not our thoughts, that His ways are higher and more perfect. The king's solution was to call for his sword. King Solomon knew what he was doing when he drew his sword. You may see what seems to be a drawn sword of death over your children; your children may be up against situations and circumstances that seem to be meant for their destruction. Your prayers to the Lord may seem to make the situation grow worse, but King Solomon's sword was not purposed to kill the boy. The sword was purposed to surface the cry of the true mother! The assignment you see before your child may look like his end, but remember, the sword is not meant to destroy him but to provoke a war cry from your spirit that will move the spirit realm on your behalf.

REBUKE THE ENEMY, REDEEM YOUR SEED

It was only a setup. The moment the enemy thought he had won, the moment the wicked mother thought she got her way, her true heart was revealed. She did not care if the boy lived; she only wanted to ensure that her friend could not have a living child if she couldn't either. This act of the king provoked the true mother to cry out for mercy upon her son. Her intercession broke through the atmosphere and pierced the heart of the king and moved him with compassion. She made a decision that demonstrated the greatest act of surrender any mother can exhibit, but this act preserved her child and ensured the enemy would not have a door to him anymore. She said, "O my lord, give her the living child, and do not kill it" (1 Kings 3:26).

We have to get to the place, moms, where we are not satisfied to share our babies with the world or the devil. We have to prefer true life for them over our own desires for them.

We have to realize that there is no halfway in the kingdom of God; they are either all in or not in at all. Half a child would not have been a truly living child. You don't want to see your son or daughter live on the fence of compromise, halfway in the church and halfway in the world, just to please or satisfy your longing for him or her. God said He would rather children be hot or cold because if they are lukewarm, as Revelation says, He would vomit them out of his mouth (Rev. 3:16). It is a scary moment, but sometimes you have to let go and say, "I would rather let the devil have them for this season than pull them apart with religion. I want their redemption to be real and them to be truly whole." This mother was willing to release her child to the enemy in order to preserve his life and future. Her love for him never waned or faded, but it drove her to make a selfless decision that would end up being the very thing that saved him.

Maybe you are a mother today in that season of release. You had to let go and seemingly lose to your adversary. Maybe it seems your son or daughter has drifted so far he or she will never come home. I challenge you not to accept the dead child as your truth and final answer. That is not the identity or future of your seed. Go to the King and plead your cause. Don't fear the grip of the enemy; it will not last. You cannot pull your child into the kingdom and from the enemy's hands; it might bring a worse outcome. Lift your voice, and allow the King to rebuke your enemy for you and redeem your seed. Only He can order that your child be removed from the influence of Satan and returned to her rightful place. Your prayers have moved Him, and His verdicts are final. His sword is not to destroy but to reveal, and the end will be life and not death! You will hold your baby again in the kingdom of God, and the devil will not have the final say. That is your child and not his. Stand on the Word, and fall at the mercy of the King. Lift your voice and let go, and trust that the King will see that your home will be restored!

I declare that the enemy must release what does not belong to him and that your sons and daughters will come back into the kingdom of light. I break off of every mother fear and worry and every deceitful lie of the enemy, and I pray that the truth of God's Word will illuminate the true identity of your child. I pray every mother's cry for mercy would shake heaven and move the heart of the King to battle on your behalf. May the Lord rebuke your enemy and restore your son or daughter to your arms! ❖

Chapter Seven
BEWARE OF THE TRAP
OF COMPARISON

⇒⇒⇒━━━━━━━━⇀

THE GAME OF comparison is such a common yet harmful trap. To compare is to examine two things to find similarities and differences. It is to measure one thing against another. As women we begin the game of comparison at an early age. We compare dresses and shoes and dolls, then bra size and boyfriends and weight, and then cooking ability and the cleanliness of our homes. When we find ourselves becoming less than successful in any area of our lives, we many times find comfort in unearthing the knowledge that someone else is less successful than us in the same area. It's the relief you experience when you walk into a friend's or neighbor's home to find piles of laundry and toys on the floor. Or it is the feeling of failure you may experience as you walk into a home that is squeaky clean and free of dust with homemade bread baking in the oven. We immediately begin to compare. It's a natural reaction.

There is nothing more vicious than the comparison that takes place at times between mothers. As mothers we have an insatiable drive to succeed at raising our children. At times we have all wrestled the drive for our kids to dress the best, achieve the best grades, score the most points, or perform the best talents. We can become guilty of measuring our success by the output in our children's lives. We may compare parenting styles, discipline styles, methods of education, and even the spirituality of our children. When we feel as if we are falling short of our potential compared with the potential of someone else, it begins a tormenting game that will drive parents to do the most absurd things. This is the breeding ground for pageant moms and academic moms and those who push their children mercilessly and behave in insane ways at sporting events just so the parents can see their children succeed over others.

We must examine the story of Elizabeth, mother of John the Baptist, in the Word of God to come to the conclusion that in order to be a Spirit-led mom who raises a child of prophetic destiny, we have to be freed from the cycle and trap of comparison. We have to release our children to be the unique individuals God has called them to be, even if it causes ridicule or potential embarrassment. Elizabeth's son, John, didn't even carry a traditional family name to begin with. I am sure it did not help her reputation when John decided that all he wanted to wear was camel hair. Imagine the social anxiety the family experienced when all John wanted to eat was locusts! Elizabeth had to overcome mother-to-mother comparison and just allow her son to be who God created him to be. We cannot fear allowing our children to wear camel hair, even if it's not the latest trend at the newest children's boutique. Standing out and being different may be the divine design for your child of purpose, and it will require you to bury your desires to fit in or be popular. Kingdom shakers were never meant to fit molds. They were created to break them. We have to allow God to do that through our children at times, and by nature that means they will not always fit in.

RADICAL GOSPEL, RADICAL LIFE

Children with unique personalities were not created to just be medicated, labeled, and tolerated. What the world diagnoses as a disorder, defect, or psychological glitch may actually be the genetic makeup of destiny. What seems undesirable or difficult to deal with in our culture may be a divine setup for kingdom influence. What significant person in biblical history or even American history ever changed the world by being normal? Yet we feel the pressure as parents to conform our children to a mold called "normal." This is the design of the enemy because normal and balanced equals comfortable and complacent in the kingdom. Jesus preached a radical gospel and lived a radical life, and He was anything but "normal." And again, as the Lord prepares for His return, God is raising up a John-the-Baptist generation that will shake our nation and the world with a style and message that will be the furthest thing from normal or balanced. God Himself said that He hates lukewarm things (Rev. 3:16). Hot or cold temperatures demand reactions, and that is how God desires for us to live our lives as believers. It starts, however, with kingdom-minded mothers who will not fear or stifle what God has ordained in their children.

My second son, Isaiah, was an unexpected treasure whose existence became known just six months or so after the birth of my firstborn, Jeremiah. My first reaction was fear and tears because I was still learning how to be a new mom. I had no idea how I would have the mechanism or strategy to double the emotional and physical strength, love, and financial load Kevin and I were carrying at the time. The second child always brings the insecurity of wondering if you could possibly love another child as much as the first and how that will all work out. Thankfully God made it known to Kevin and me that He was in control and that this was no accident, as the world may have jokingly said. This child was divinely ordered by God in His way and His timing. One commonality of mothers who are raising children of prophetic destiny is this: God will make sure you are not in control on purpose, and early on. This was the case with Isaiah. His name was given by God with the scripture from Isaiah 6:8. The Lord asked, "Whom shall I send, and who will go for us?" Isaiah then answered "Here am I. Send me." God made it clear from the time that Isaiah was in the womb that this child would go for Him. God also spoke to us that as the prophet Isaiah demonstrated radical obedience in his life, our son Isaiah would be a son of radical obedience.

Looking back now, I realize I should have braced myself for the opposition of the enemy surrounding Isaiah's life. As can be seen in the lives of kingdom mothers such as Jochebed, the enemy never underestimates the potential packed in a small little bundle of joy, even at birth. One of the worst mistakes a mother can make is to underestimate the mark of God upon her seed. We cannot simply view our children for who they are in the present moment, but we must continually be aware of the fullness of who they can and will become. Don't be blinded by the bundle of cuddly cuteness they are because the enemy sees well beyond that. It is plain and simple: the devil fears godly seed. He sees the mark of God and attacks early and unmercifully. This is why we see infanticide in Exodus and Matthew around the birth of Moses and then of Jesus. Satan's intention has always been destruction and the silencing of the voice of the prophet, and he will not play fair or nice. Therefore we cannot play fair or nice either, Mom. Matthew 10:16 says we must be as wise as a serpent, cunning and undetected, yet as harmless as a dove.

SURRENDERING TO THE WISDOM
OF THE HOLY SPIRIT

Isaiah has been the most precious blessing of my life. However, it wasn't very long at all after his birth that Isaiah began to display what a unique individual he was created to be. His thought processing, perception, social skills, and general emotional makeup were unique and unlike anyone else in the family. In the natural his uniqueness showed in various ways, such as extreme sensory challenges. He would have intense emotional responses to certain clothing materials and even vomit food that had certain textures. He was at times very resistant to touch and affection, and the Wallace family is a very affectionate family! He had sleeping-pattern issues where he would fall asleep so quickly it was almost like narcolepsy, yet he would wake up at 3:00 a.m. and stay awake for hours. He was sensitive to noise and had no tolerance for disorder or change and transition. A simple schedule change would produce panic attacks, and making decisions seemed for him like a life-or-death choice every time. We couldn't even take him shopping at a toy store because the options and pressure to make a choice would send him over the deep end. He would obsess over one type of toy and focus only on it for every birthday and Christmas. First it was Thomas the Train, and then it became LEGOs and Star Wars. Molding and disciplining Isaiah became the daily challenge of my life, and there were days when all I could do was curl up in a ball in my bed and weep hot tears of failure. I begged and pleaded with God for grace and wisdom because I did not know how to handle my own son, and my own son seemed to grow more and more distant from me in his heart because he felt so misunderstood.

I remember staying awake all night with Isaiah many

nights because he couldn't and wouldn't sleep. I tried to reason with him, threaten him, and plead with him, all to no avail. One night in particular I finally wrapped his two-and-a-half-year-old frame in my arms and just began to war in prayer, praying in tongues over him until he fell asleep limp in my arms. What else was I to do? That is when the light bulb clicked on for me in my spirit. The Holy Spirit spoke to me that night and said, "I am the best parent. I understand what you don't because I formed him Myself." In that moment I realized what I had been trying to do on my own to understand and parent Isaiah was miserably failing. All my parenting books and psychological training did nothing to help me because they were the wrong instruction manuals. Those wonderful theories were written by a theorist who didn't even know Isaiah's name, let alone the number of hairs on his head.

I stopped looking to my own knowledge and strength and surrendered to the wisdom and strategy of God.

All along I had the best resource I could need; I had the ever-present help and Comforter, the Holy Spirit. Religious mind-sets broke off me as the Holy Spirit whispered to me. I realized the Holy Spirit wasn't just moving in the altars of our church, but He was also present with me as a mother, just as He is with all mothers. He was sitting beside me on the floor as I sat up with Isaiah all night, and He was with me when I cried in my bedroom. He saw me try to get Isaiah to eat his green beans. He was there the entire time, saying, "If you would just allow Me, I can show you how to train Isaiah. I know how he is wired, and I know the plans I have for his future." I was as stubborn as a man who refuses to ask for instructions when he is assembling something for his child.

I had the builder Himself, yet I tried to seek guidance from outside distant sources. When I realized this, my parenting of Isaiah changed. I could not use the same methods and strategies I had used for Jeremiah. They were two different yet incredible individuals. I stopped looking to my own knowledge and strength and surrendered to the wisdom and strategy of God. Every day I would pray, "God, today show me how to handle Isaiah. Give me strategy, and I will obey."

It was little things that produced big results in Isaiah's life. It started with my first accepting the same truth that Elizabeth must have had to confront and accept with her son John the Baptist: My child was made to be different from other children. I was to shape and sharpen him, not try to conform him or compare him to others. He was a mold breaker. This is how God made my child on purpose. This was not a disorder, mistake, or handicap. This was a divine design for a divine purpose. I had to open my eyes to the gift of Isaiah's uniqueness and help him manage what he had been given. Just because he was unique and chosen did not mean he was born knowing what was best for him or how to handle the unique gifts he had been given. Look at Mary and Joseph with Christ. During His childhood He went missing for three days to teach in the temple (Luke 2:41–52). Can you imagine the stress Mary and Joseph endured and the inconvenience of repeating the journey to Jerusalem to search for him? When Mary found Jesus, He didn't even seem to understand what the big deal was! Sometimes unique callings on children bring unique challenges to parents. Isaiah was desperate for guidance and training, but he did not need criticism or conformity.

CHILDREN OF PROPHETIC PURPOSE

Isaiah's keen sensory perception made him an extremely sensitive person in all areas of his life. For example, even now he can smell what is undetectable to the rest of the family, even to the point of determining a missing ingredient from a recipe. He can also sense and see things in the spirit realm that we cannot always perceive. His natural sensitivity is not to torture him, but it serves to give him hypersensitivity to the Spirit.

I first realized just how open his spiritual eyes and ears were one day after a very disturbing but real spiritual experience Kevin and I had in our home. One night after the kids were fast asleep, we were working in our front office by our front door. Kevin and I saw a large dark shadow come through the crack of the front door and whisk quickly by us down the hallway. I thought my eyes were playing tricks on me until we heard a loud thumping on the office wall, the wall that connected to my oldest son, Jeremiah's bedroom. Kevin and I didn't even say a word to each other. We both jumped up and darted to Jeremiah's room. The thumping on the wall was the sound of Jeremiah kicking as he gasped to breathe in his bed. At the time he was not even in kindergarten yet. Kevin began to speak in tongues and rebuke the devil, and peace came over Jeremiah as he drifted back to sleep. We looked at each other in disbelief, not understanding exactly what had just attacked our son or if this had happened before when we weren't aware. Could this have been why Isaiah, who shared a room with him, would wake up so much at night?

The next morning I was getting ready in front of my bathroom mirror while Isaiah was playing in the bathtub behind me. I was thinking about what had happened to Jeremiah, and I asked the Lord this question in my mind but not out loud. I prayed, "What was that? Was it a spirit, and what spirit was it?" It was as if Isaiah heard the thoughts of my mind or the Holy Spirit Himself was answering me through him. Isaiah said to me, "Mom, what does A-S-T-H-M-A spell? Azzz...what?" I almost passed out on the floor! Isaiah was seeing the word *asthma* in his mind and spirit. He heard the answer of the Lord, and he was three! Whatever attacked Jeremiah was affecting his breathing, and I believe the Lord was revealing it was an assignment of the enemy that brought an asthma attack upon him. Isaiah heard what I couldn't. This was just the first of several times that Isaiah would see or hear something from the Spirit and not even realize what he was doing.

When Isaiah was nine, our church experienced a lot of growth through God-given vision, and this always brings financial needs. Kevin was weighed down with the stress of building campaigns and mission plans, and we were in need of a financial miracle. Isaiah told us that God told him to give all of his birthday money in a special offering we were about to receive for an orphanage we had committed to build in Guatemala.

"Are you sure that's what God said, Isaiah?" Kevin would ask in the days leading up to the special Sunday. We just couldn't believe Isaiah wanted to put it all in the offering, but sure enough he did. Several times in the weeks after Isaiah gave, he would tell his dad, "The Lord is going to give our church a million dollars." And after a while it began to agitate my stressed-out husband as to why Isaiah was saying it so much. He said it four separate times! God rebuked Kevin one day and said, "Isaiah has faith for a miracle like that because he gave Me everything he had." Sure enough, just a few weeks later, God gave our church the largest financial miracle we had ever received in our history as pastors, and it even exceeded Isaiah's declaration of one million dollars. Overnight we were debt free and able to increase our kingdom advancement because of the obedience of one unique child. Isaiah had prophesied our miracle.

Isaiah also demonstrated keen intellectual ability. He could remember everything in great detail. He was a master builder and designer, as we learned with his LEGO obsession. There was a season that Isaiah became obsessed with expressing the Word of God through his passion for LEGOs. On his own he created LEGO set after LEGO set that displayed the stories of God's Word. From David and Goliath to the priests in the temple and even the Crucifixion, Isaiah crafted them all! He called them his Bible creations, and he would amaze our house guests with his attention to detail and biblical accuracy. He was sharing the gospel in a very unconventional way, and he did it all by himself! His creativity also came out in a love for music. He began teaching himself to play the piano; he could play just by hearing a song.

Isaiah would pray with his eyes open at home and at church. It was strange to me to see him looking around during prayer, so one day I said to Isaiah, "You need to close your eyes while you pray."

Very quickly and matter-of-factly Isaiah asked, "Why do I have to close my eyes while I pray? I like to keep them open." The Lord convicted my heart and said to let him pray how he wants to pray, that he is looking and seeing things. Isaiah has seen angels and has had open visions.

During one service a dear saint in our church saw an angel behind my husband as he preached. No one was aware of what had been reported other than my husband, the individual, and me. Isaiah wasn't even with us at the time. In the same service Isaiah was coloring in the floor with friends, and all of a sudden he jumped up and ran over to me during the preaching. He described the same angel behind his father that the dear saint had just told me about. He saw it as he was coloring on the floor by the altar.

On another occasion Isaiah even foresaw the death of our dear pastor emeritus just weeks before he died. He ran over to me during service one day and said, "Mom, I just saw an angel over top of Brother Kelley. It was pulling up on the shoulders of his shirt like he was trying to take Brother Kelley with him, but Brother Kelley was pulling back." Brother Kelley had just told my husband that he did not want to die yet. He wanted to be here when the Rapture took place. It was just a few short weeks later that the Lord did call him home.

Why am I saying all of this? To encourage a mom who has a child who is classified as "different." What the world would later call a handicap was actually a divine setup by God for a child of prophetic purpose. What prophet in Scripture ever lived up to the profile of "normal"? Hosea had to marry and remain faithful to a prostitute (Hosea 1:2). Jeremiah tried to be silent and normal, but the call of God on his life pushed him as if his bones were on fire (Jer. 20:9). Samuel was dropped off at the temple around age five and slept near the holy place (1 Sam. 1). When a child appears different in the natural realm, it is often because he is different in the spiritual realm.

THE CHILD WHO BREAKS THE MOLD

My favorite example of the abnormal profile of a prophetic child is John the Baptist, son of Elizabeth. In fact, God took me to this story during the early years of raising Isaiah. John the Baptist represents what I classify as the clothed-in-camel-hair child, the child who was born to break molds. Now that I have partially raised my own clothed-in-camel-hair child, I can spot these children a mile away. I can see it in their eyes as they process the world around them. They are the children who are born to be intentionally different and to stand out for a purpose. They are the children who are meant to challenge patterns and confront the complacent, even if it is their own mother and father, as it was in my case. Our society doesn't know how to classify children such as that or even how to mold them. We resort to labels and diagnoses to make them easier to deal with, and we medicate them, at times merely for the sake of convenience. Could we be stifling and disabling the unique makeup they were given to become conduits to the realm of heaven? Have we become so self-absorbed with the expectations of our culture that we don't want to be inconvenienced with the challenge of raising a child like John? I am a living testimony that the challenge is worth the effort, and the fruit of such a unique child of God is priceless. I can't say it enough: one life can change an entire generation! One prophetic voice can turn the tide of a society. One little boy named John prepared the way for Messiah to save humanity, but it took a mom like Elizabeth to shape a child like John.

As mothers, let's put ourselves in the position of Elizabeth. To begin with, she carried shame and disappointment because she could not conceive a child. This was the ultimate indictment for a woman in her time. She wasn't barren because she did something wrong, although many times she may have wondered. She was barren because she did something right. It was not denial from God; it was a divine setup. It was not punishment, but timing. We've heard it said before: delay is not denial. She was preserved and prepped for the miraculous events that would surround who Jesus said was the greatest man to walk the earth (Matt. 11:11). Elizabeth was not destined to have *a* child, but *the* child, the one who would turn the hearts of the fathers to the children and the hearts of the children to the fathers. Being the mother of such a child always carries a price tag called process. It's like a pearl of great price or a dia-

One little boy named John prepared the way for Messiah to save humanity, but it took a mom like Elizabeth to shape a child like John.

mond in the rough. Most things with great value are not easily obtained or required. With a child such as John, it took a difficult process of barrenness and reproach to validate the miracle of his birth. It took his father's tongue being unable to speak to reveal the plan of God. It took unusual clothing and an unusual message to achieve extraordinary results. It cost Elizabeth some peace, some sleep, and her reputation to be John's mother.

With the birth of a child such as John there is almost always opposition, opposition from the enemy and from society to silence what confronts us and troubles our complacency. In this story there was even opposition within the family. Zechariah at first couldn't believe it. Then the relatives didn't want to agree with the name God had given the boy. They wanted him to conform to the pattern of his father. Elizabeth had to stand up to her own family, who could not understand the child she had given birth to. She exemplifies a commonality of mothers who birth a child of prophetic purpose: pain is unavoidable. We see this even in the mother of Christ Himself. Mary was given the incredible honor of birthing the Messiah, yet she received the prophecy that a sword would pierce her soul (Luke 2:35). In other words, the honor and glory of being the Messiah's mother carried the price tag of pain. What mother, other than Mary, could have survived watching her son endure the cross? Pain and struggle are inevitable and undeniable for a mother who will sharpen and release a child of prophetic promise.

Elizabeth's pain of barrenness was simply the pathway to participate in a miracle. I believe it took that level of desperation and surrender on the part of Elizabeth to raise a child like John according to the plan that God had for him. If she hadn't been so desperate, she may not have been so willing to surrender him. She might have taken matters into her own hands. As with Hannah, the mother of Samuel, the place of desperation Elizabeth was in was a place of surrender that allowed her to conform to the radical plan of God. Everyone wanted to step in and give John his identity and purpose, but Elizabeth didn't care about pleasing people anymore. She had already overcome the sting of social rejection. She wasn't even worried about pleasing her husband, for she had already overcome the obstacle of not being able to please him. She cared only about pleasing the One who gave her this child, and God spoke and acted on her behalf.

Why was John born in the first place and given to Elizabeth and Zechariah? The promise of John's birth came during Zechariah's turn to serve in the temple of God. It was his turn to go into the holy of holies. It was in the very presence of God, before the veil, that the concept of John was spoken before the form of John was created (Luke 1:8–17). God created him to fill a purpose. God doesn't try to find purpose for those He has created as if purpose is an afterthought. God creates His children to fill specific purposes on the earth. We must instill this concept in our children from birth. Children are created to spend more time fulfilling purpose than searching for it. They are designed for their assigned place in the kingdom of God, and they will not find complete fulfillment outside of that assignment.

More than just a purpose, John came as an answer to prayer. I am sure it is safe to say that Zechariah and Elizabeth had cried out to God for a child. But more specifically, at the time the angel appeared to Zechariah, the Word says the people were praying outside the temple while the priest was praying inside the temple (Luke 1:10). They were crying out for atonement and redemption from the judgment of sin. God's answer was a child, a voice, a prophetic voice that would prepare the way for the true Redeemer. Moses was an answer to the cry of God's people in the Book of Exodus. Samuel was an answer to the prayers of Hannah and the answer to the demise of the spiritual leadership of God's people. We must view our precious little ones as an answer to a problem, not the source of one. They are an answer to prayer, fully equipped in every way to fill a specific, valuable purpose in the kingdom and plan of God. Don't be afraid of that purpose, even if it is to destroy a mold.

I declare you are released, woman of God, from any fear of your child being different. I pray the fear of man would be broken off of your life and the pressure to be normal would be removed from your shoulders. I pray the Lord would silence those who speak against the destiny of your children and remove the influence of those who would mold your children to cultural expectations instead of their kingdom purposes. I pray a release from labels that do not line up with true identity, and that grace would be given for every challenge you may be facing raising your clothed-in-camel-hair child. I pray that You, O Lord, would release divine strategy into the heart of every mother as she aligns with Your kingdom purpose over her home! ❖

Chapter Eight
STOP COPING, AND START SHAPING

》》》•————————————•

ONE OF MY greatest concerns for those in this rising generation is that we have fostered a mentality that their purpose is within their own decision-making ability and that their
destiny is whatever they want or choose it to be. Although we
have been given the power of choice, its abuse leads to a life
lacking fulfillment and direction. The only way to find what
fulfills us and what we were created to do is by seeking our
maker. I can testify that sometimes what we think we want
is not really what is best for us. I spent a large portion of my
young adult life pursuing a career as a medical doctor, not a
minister or mother. Only in the surrender of my heart and
will to the Lord did I find the path of peace and the destiny for
my life. I had no idea that my plans would have left me empty
and that God had such an exciting path in mind for me. I was
made specifically for what I do right now, and I find fulfilment
in that every day of my life! I thank God for Proverbs 16:9: "A
man's heart devises his way, but the LORD directs his steps."

We have failed to teach this generation what Jeremiah 17:9
teaches: "The heart is more deceitful than all things." Instead,
we have coined detrimental phrases such as "Follow your
heart" rather than "Follow the Spirit." This generation lives
in the realm of desires and feelings instead of walking by the
Spirit of discernment and truth. Total freedom of choice in
their lives has produced a sense of aimlessness and insecurity,
like a ship with no compass and no intended destination. In

this day 80 percent of college students change their major at least once; most of them will change it three times before settling on a degree.[1] Statistics say that 52 percent of employees are unhappy at work, meaning they are not satisfied in the place they are investing most of their time each day.[2] Suicide is the third-leading cause of death of fifteen- to twenty-four-year-olds.[3] That is entirely too many young people lacking inward knowledge of the purpose behind their future and life. I believe a sense of aimlessness is one of the leading causes for these statistics. We have followed our own passions unchecked by the Spirit and missed the target that we were created to hit. That is what sin is after all—missing the mark. Without a vision, the Word says, people perish (Prov. 29:18). A vision is what provides direction. Aimless living is empty living.

What can cause an arrow in the natural to miss the mark? Defects or incomplete steps in the shaping process. It is the same in the spirit realm. The more we allow ourselves to choose the path we want without the guidance and shaping of God, the more we will move away from our destiny and into a lifestyle of empty living, as an arrow that has fallen to the ground instead of hitting the bull's-eye. That lack of fulfillment can be what reveals to us that we don't really know ourselves the way our maker does. False statements such as "You can be anything you want to be" leave out the truth that only through Christ and the anointing can we accomplish unlimited success. When we are anointed by God, it strengthens us to accomplish what we could not do in the natural realm on our own. The anointing is the supernatural touch of God upon our lives and the lives of our children to overcome in every situation. It is the ability that God places upon us to accomplish the assignments He places before us. Operating within that anointing brings grace and fulfillment.

Attempting to find success in our own efforts and outside of the grace of the anointing will limit us to our natural ability and limitations, and it can produce frustration and dissatisfaction. It will require more effort with limited success.

The anointing is for specific purposes. The concept of destiny as some mystical discovery that only the chosen find is such a fallacy, yet we teach it to our children. Destiny is simply the result of choices, and every choice either leads us closer to or further away from the target God purposes for us to hit. Our full potential is reached when we tap into the purpose that our designer created us for, not when we chase after dreams that we were never intended to fulfill. We must instill in our children that they were created full of potential and purpose that can only be unlocked through Christ. They must learn to surrender their will to the will of the Father, who ultimately knows what will satisfy them.

Our children cannot be forced into their future, but they certainly need to be guided. God gave specific directions to Manoah's wife as she raised Samson so she could make choices for him before he was mature enough to make them for himself (Judg. 13:3–5). Hannah made a heavy choice for Samuel when she committed him to the work of the temple (1 Sam. 1). Abraham made a life-altering choice for Isaac when he climbed up Mount Moriah to offer him as a sacrifice to the Lord (Gen. 22). These parents did not enforce these choices because they were their own dreams for their children. They were each following the commands and desires of the Lord, and they did not put it up for household debate or discussion. Mom, you have to be comfortable in the driver's seat at times and realize your babies aren't born knowing how to make mature choices. That is why they have you. Boundaries set in place by the Word and by the Holy Spirit may not always be desirable to your child, but they will be profitable to the success of your child's future. The destiny of your child starts with you, and that is a heavy responsibility.

THE COMPASS OF THE HOLY SPIRIT

We have heard it said that God is not as concerned with our comfort as He is our character. We need to adopt that kind of agape love, mothers, that shakes us out of the selfishness of wanting to be our children's friend over being the steward of their lives. Those in this generation are crying out for boundaries and guidance; they need to know that they matter. We need to equip them not with a map we have designed ourselves, but with a compass called the leading of the Spirit that will guide them to God's plan, no matter how many twists or turns they take. A map is a rigid plan that can become obsolete over time, but a compass will endure over time and even through change. It will always point north no matter where you go. If our children can gain a spiritual compass that always points them to God, they can find their way back to His purpose even if they get lost or take a wrong turn.

John the Baptist was created to fulfill a prophetic purpose, and it was decided before he was even conceived (Luke 1:15–17). It was determined and set in motion before he could even speak. His life was not about finding purpose, but about fulfilling purpose. God silenced the one who spoke against it and shamed those who tried to give him a family name over his true identity (Luke 1:19–20, 59–62). John had an internal compass given by God called the leading of the Spirit, and it drove him from the comfort of his home to the wilderness (Luke 1:80).

After overcoming the shame of barrenness and then those who wanted to deny her the right to name her own son, she now had the "weird" child who stood out in the crowd. We can only imagine how frustrated Elizabeth was at times, and many of us can relate to her. What must Elizabeth have thought when her child refused her home cooking and cried for locusts with wild honey. She must have lost her temper or shed a few tears when he refused to wear her beautiful handmade garments because he thought camel hair was cool and he couldn't handle the feel of cotton (Matt. 3:4). How did she respond when John never wanted to play with the other kids in the neighborhood, but instead he desired to spend long days alone in the wilderness? From this information it is safe to say that if John had been born in this day and age, he would have been called antisocial and diagnosed with every disorder known to man, from sensory processing disorder to maybe even bipolar disorder. I am sure they would have thrown in some vitamin deficiency issue for his choice of diet. They probably would have tagged on a stress or anxiety disorder because of his daily message of repent or burn. He would have been highly medicated before he even reached kindergarten.

Please understand that I don't say all of this to deny the true disorders that are diagnosed among children in our society today. As I discussed earlier, my own son was diagnosed with about three to four pages of complications. I am saying this to encourage the mother of a clothed-in-camel-hair child. Maybe all those disorders are just a part of the unique makeup it will take for your child to make a significant impact in the world. We have to highlight the positive aspects of such challenges and train our children to

When you are given a child with much potential, the requirements upon you will be great.

103

manage what may be perceived as negative. Talk to your child's physician, but I believe medication should be reserved for conditions in which assistance in managing them is truly needed, not for the convenience of making the training and parenting of our unique children less of a burden or headache. There is not an easy road in raising a clothed-in-camel-hair child. However, if God gave that baby to you, it is because you have what it takes to unlock the potential inside of him.

We cannot let these children remain unbridled and undisciplined as sympathy for their uniqueness. It is quite the opposite. An even greater responsibility rests upon their shoulders to learn how to live a life of surrender to God and obedience to His leading. "To whom much is given, of him much shall be required" (Luke 12:48). Their diagnoses cannot become excuses. It will simply be a challenge, and that may seem unfair at times. Favor, Mom, isn't always fair. When you are given a child with much potential, the requirements upon you will be great. For those of you with the gift of a clothed-in-camel-hair child, you may cry many tears and experience pain and rejection. You will have to hold on to the Holy Spirit for direction and guidance because there is not a manual for your task and assignment. Even Elizabeth was filled with the Holy Spirit as John was in her womb (Luke 1:41), and Mom, you will need the infilling of the Holy Spirit too!

EQUIPPING INSTEAD OF ACCOMMODATING

I shared earlier about some of the challenges our son Isaiah faced. In parenting him, I had to stop caring what the latest parenting fad was. I had to ignore the temptation to compare him with other children and to accommodate everything he desired to find the easy road in this journey. I had to discipline myself daily to walk with an ear tuned to the windowsill of heaven. The Holy Spirit Himself guided and directed me in practical daily strategies for molding and shaping Isaiah to become the arrow God created Him to be. The Holy Spirit reminded me over and over again that God designed Isaiah and had the best instruction and assembly manual that could be offered for my precious baby boy. I had to consult the maker and not my emotions or fears. I began to experience Holy Spirit nudges and Holy Spirit whispers in my daily walk as a mother. I learned to intercede while doing laundry, cleaning, and driving to and from school. I had some of the most impactful encounters with God while sitting on my living room floor or in my kitchen. We as moms are sometimes too distracted and too weighed down to even notice His whispers, but you are not alone, Mom. God sees, and God cares. Just invite Him to be a daily part of the parenting process.

Even before I had the knowledge of Isaiah's diagnoses, my journey started with radical and sometimes ridiculous-sounding instructions that led to unprecedented impact. For example, the Lord dealt with my heart about Isaiah being a finicky eater. Isaiah had serious texture issues and only wanted to eat a few select foods. God asked me one day to stop accommodating his requests and to train him to eat what his body needed. It was easier by far to feed Isaiah chicken nuggets for every meal, but it was not what was best for him or his future. The Holy Spirit whispered, "What if I send him to China one day? He needs to learn to eat what is put in front of him." And so the battle ensued. I fixed Isaiah, as well as the rest of the tribe, a plate of whatever was prepared for dinner that day. Isaiah had to eat a set number of bites of every food, even if the texture made him gag. We learned to say how thankful we were for our food when it was put before us instead of issuing any word of complaint. I introduced some foods to him five or six times, even if he didn't like them, and to my surprise he began to develop a taste for them. He didn't grimace as much over time, but it did take a long time. He learned to get over or at least manage his food preferences. He learned to eat for survival and health and not always for taste. I can, by the grace of God, testify today that as a teenager Isaiah is one of my most adventurous eaters, especially when it comes to food from other cultures. He may not like everything, but he has no fear of trying it! I praise God when I hear others comment on how he will eat anything! I see him try new things and clean his plate. Moms, we spend too much time accommodating things we are supposed to be eradicating in our children's lives. They cannot self-parent. Many choices are not theirs to make, such as the food they eat. When true hunger hits, a child will eat and be grateful for what is on his plate. Convenience is many times the enemy of true training and shaping.

Another time that the Holy Spirit nudged me concerning Isaiah was about his life-controlling obsession with order. We did not know at the time, but he was diagnosed with mild obsessive-compulsive disorder (OCD). Isaiah loved trains and was known for getting upset if a track or a train was out of order. He would throw himself on the floor and cry uncontrollably over one wrong move on his set. This was true for almost anything in Isaiah's life. He wanted a high level of control over the world around him. However, this was an ideology that had to be confronted. Isaiah would never be able to control the entire world around him, and if this desire for control remained unaddressed, it could lead to a very miserable and frustrating future. Order is not always achievable in this thing we call life. Isaiah had to learn he could desire and aim for order and structure, but if life ever threw him a curve ball, he needed to be able to roll with the punches and manage the tendency to lash out. Being a child in a preacher's home, Isaiah had to learn to be patient and flexible with a schedule we could not always control.

One day I walked into Isaiah's room, and the Holy Spirit said to me, "Move one of his trains out of order." I think I had a panic attack at that moment because I knew the tornado of emotions that would come from my little one if I did that. As a mom I also experienced anxiety when I knew Isaiah was about to throw a fit. Everyone was afraid to touch his trains. I didn't understand why the Holy Spirit was saying it, but I had learned already to obey and trust, so I moved his favorite train. Just a few moments passed, and Isaiah came bouncing down the hall to his room. As soon as his eyes locked on the train table, he realized that the unthinkable had been done! He immediately crashed to the floor in an array of emotions. He uttered unintelligible words, and he pounded and cried. "Now what?" I thought. The Holy Spirit said, "Now love him through it, but do not compromise." My first reaction was to put the train back so all would be peaceful again. But I had to remember that although it may have been easier in the moment, it would not have been best for his future.

I got on the floor with Isaiah and wrapped my arms around him. He wasn't even focused on the love I was trying to offer in that moment, but I spoke these words to him: "Isaiah, it is going to be OK. It is OK if a train gets out of order sometimes. Life will get out of order sometimes, and we are going to learn to deal with how you are feeling right now."

"I know!" he explained. "I just want it to be like it was."

I responded and said, "I understand, Isaiah, but right now I want you to breathe and deal with how you are feeling. It can't always be the way you want it, and I want you to trust me." We cried, objected, and talked until some minor form of calm came over him. I distracted him with something else and placed the train back in order.

I repeated this several times over the next few weeks and months until Isaiah began to trust more of what I said. I would always tell him that the train could be put back in order, just not now. I felt like a mom who was torturing her child, but the Lord let me know that day that I was training him. I was training him to overcome tendencies he had that would have hindered his future. He eventually realized that the world did not fall apart if his trains were moved, and a peace came to him when he realized he could survive it. It was not an unknown fear anymore; it was a present reality that he had the strength to deal with. God let me know it was better to learn to cope in the arms of a loving mother than in the uncertainty of the world.

We spend far too much time accommodating instead of training and equipping. Convenience is the enemy to a mother because there is nothing convenient about shaping a child. Whatever is easy is not always right! Love says, "I love you too much to leave you this way or for you to deal with life by yourself." Isaiah and I developed such a bond out of moments like that. I had to be patient and loving and calm to make it through, but it was necessary because I needed to be more concerned about his future than the comfort of my present. There were times I would just hold him and rock him and pray in the Holy Ghost, but through this he did learn to trust me even when it frustrated him. He learned to manage reactions that once seemed uncontrollable and harness the unique attributes he had been given when he needed to. We did not break or bend the strength of those attributes, but he had to learn to be in the driver's seat of his own will, desires, and emotions with the help of the Holy Spirit. A child that does not learn to manage himself is like a horse that has not been trained for its rider. It can have all the potential in the world, but its strengths will become hazards instead of gifts without a bridle and rein.

RISE UP AND DECLARE
GOD'S IDENTITY FOR YOUR CHILD

To make years worth of stories into a shortened version, Isaiah began to grow, and God began to shape how I shaped him. It was several years later that we saw a team of specialists at our pediatrician's recommendation. After careful and extensive observations from physical and occupational therapists, psychologists, and a developmental specialist, the reality of what I had been wrestling with as a mother became clear. Kevin and I received a three- to four-page diagnostic report of our son, with diagnoses ranging from attention deficit/hyperactivity disorder (ADHD) to OCD and anxiety disorders to the unthinkable—autism spectrum disorder (ASD). I was stunned, to say the least, and I was called into a meeting with the pediatric developmental specialist. After he read the paperwork and observed Isaiah for most of the morning, he asked me the strangest question: "What did you do?"

"What do you mean?" I asked.

He replied, "Your son shows every physical sign of an ASD, from his bone structure to his play methods. However, socially and emotionally it doesn't line up. He makes eye contact with me, and I literally watched him manage himself during play in a situation that should have caused him stress. I have never seen a child learn to manage their condition!" Again he asked, "What did you do? Whatever you did, you really need to share it in our parents of autistic children group. Whatever you did is monumental."

THE WARRIOR WE CALL MOM

I was stunned, to say the least. "I didn't even know my son was autistic, Doctor. I knew something was different, and you are not going to believe this, but I just prayed and asked God what to do to help him. I never allowed him to become his condition, and I always treated him and shaped him like a normal child." There was an awkward silence, and then the doctor discussed doing more tests to try to figure this situation out. But I simply asked, "Does he need treatment in any way? Because if he doesn't, we are done with doctor appointments." He said we were released and that Isaiah had received everything that he could have needed.

Needless to say, the drive home was filled with tears and then laughter and praise. First of all I felt such guilt that all this time my son had a condition, several conditions, and I was totally unaware. Then I praised God because I was unaware, because if I had been aware, I would have caved in to his condition and possibly never challenged Isaiah to overcome such challenges at an early age. I could not believe God had helped our family win a battle we didn't even know we were fighting! That is Spirit-led parenting! It is proof that it's not about what we know as mothers but about what He knows as creator! To this day Isaiah has never had to take one prescription for any of his conditions, and he has never had to be in one special class at school or have any exceptions made for him. In fact, he is a regular honor roll student. There are times the enemy rears his head, and Isaiah and I have to go back to the battleground of dealing with self and tendencies. However, with trust, lots of love and patience, and prayer he has always overcome. Isaiah is one of the most unique and spiritually in-tune children I have ever met. His unique sensory perception and mind-set allow him to hear and see in the spirit in such a unique way.

I often wonder if our society has chosen a pill bottle for coping instead of a prayer life for strategies for shaping. I realize and have personally seen instances where medication is absolutely needed in the life of a child, sometimes for focus and emotional support for a season. That being said, more often than not we dull things we are supposed to sharpen in our children in the name of convenience. This may seem like a harsh statement, but I am convinced many children with mild cases of OCD and sensory disorders and even ASD and ADHD are just wired differently to walk in a unique calling and purpose. I believe these clothed-in-camel-hair children were meant to be shaped to see and hear in a prophetic way for our culture. I pray for godly mothers such as Elizabeth to rise up and declare that the identities of their children are God's decision, and labeling is not an option. Elizabeth would not allow others (society) to name her little one. His name was John; it was different and unconventional. You, Mom, should not allow others to attach labels and names to the identity of your child. Even if she has a true condition, it does not have to be woven into her identity! If Elizabeth could have written a book for us, I can only imagine the challenges she faced with a child like John who walked in the Spirit from the womb. Elizabeth knew that John was not hers but a gift from God. She knew he was created for a specific purpose.

The return of Christ is near, and those in this generation have a similar mandate to John. They must prepare the way of the Lord. He is raising up not one prophetic voice, as He did in the time of Christ, but a generation of prophetic voices that will shake the nations with the message of the Messiah. It is a generation that picks up the mantles of former generals of the faith that have fallen to the ground, just as John took on the hairy mantle of Elijah. Elijah was the only other prophet recorded in Scripture to wear a garment of hair. Jewish tradition even teaches that Elijah's mantle was kept at the right side of the altar of incense, which is where Zechariah stood when the Lord spoke to him concerning his son, John.[4] John could have possibly worn the garment Elijah wore, literally completing what Christ prophesied when He said one would come in the Spirit and power of Elijah. Oh, that our children would pick up fallen mantles that our generation has allowed to sit as monuments. A mantle of camel hair represents a hide or covering that can adjust to changing and adverse temperatures. It is a tough skin; it is a covering that keeps the temperature inside steady when temperatures are extreme on the outside. A camel dwells in desert temperatures of record highs and frigid lows. The clothing John wore that may have been criticized was actually what preserved and kept him as he wandered in the wilderness. His unique mantle was his equipment. That is what we must clothe our children in, mothers: a tough skin or covering that keeps them grounded and steadfast in a rapidly changing culture, a garment that protects them from the scourging heat of the enemy's arrows and keeps them from freezing in frigid atmospheres of religion and complacency! Camel hair is a steadfast covering that is internally consistent even in an externally changing environment.

I pray for godly mothers such as Elizabeth to rise up and declare that the identities of their children are God's decision, and labeling is not an option.

God is calling our children to look different, eat differently, talk differently, and sound differently than the surrounding culture—a generation that will break the molds of religion and complacency and lift a sound that cannot be silenced, a generation whose voice will be the trumpet sounding the arrival of the Messiah to turn the hearts of the fathers back to the children and the children to the fathers. In order to raise up a generation of clothed-in-camel-hair children, God is looking for an army of moms similar to Elizabeth who don't care about popular opinion and who will not play the game of comparison. He is looking for mothers who truly see the potential of the children they have been entrusted with and who will walk by the Spirit daily. He is looking for mothers who have already survived the pain of the process and are surrendered to the Lord. Rise up, Elizabeth, and allow the Lord to make your hands a weapon! Shape your arrow as God leads, and watch the Spirit of God shake a community and a nation by your obedience!

I declare the unveiling of a John the Baptist generation that will prepare the way for the return of Christ. May they cry aloud and spare not and break the bondage of religion over the church by breaking every mold. I declare our children will remain steadfast and constant in their faith, even as the world around them shifts and changes. May they refuse to remain silent in and speak the truth to combat the deception of their culture, and may they be unshakable and unstoppable for His kingdom! ❖

Chapter Nine
RELEASING YOUR CHILDREN:
AN ACT OF WORSHIP

MY HUSBAND, KEVIN, and I began pastoring our church when we were relatively young. We were both just twenty-two when we came to the outskirts of Chattanooga, Tennessee. Jeremiah was fifteen months old at the time, and I was eight months pregnant with Isaiah. I have no idea why, but with the birth of every child we saw transition in our personal lives, our ministry, or our church. It was as if we were pregnant in the Spirit every time we were pregnant in the natural. I am sure some of you can relate. With the approaching birth of Isaiah it was both a physical and spiritual transition, and I found myself in a new place surrounded by new people and in a new role that I had never filled before.

THAT PLACE OF DESPERATION—
A BIRTHING GROUND FOR GOD'S STRATEGY

Trying to find my identity as a new mom of two little boys, as well as the wife of the new pastor of a small church, was no easy challenge. I was just as equipped to be a pastor's wife as I was to be a professional bull rider, and I have never ridden a bull in my life! I didn't know what I was doing or what I was getting into. I had watched my grandmother growing up—she was a faithful Methodist pastor's wife and organ player for all of my childhood—but I didn't play the piano and certainly did not exude her grace and patience.

I felt like a fish out of water in so many ways, and balance was such a difficult thing to find. I was approached about leading the women's ministry at the church, and I laugh out loud now as I remember how it all unfolded. One of the deacons of the church came to me and put a checkbook in my hand and said, "Here is the ladies' ministries checkbook. There are a few hundred dollars in the account. Someone's gotta do it, and I reckon it's going to be you." And that was it. That was my introduction to women's ministry.

All I had encountered up until that point was traditional women's ministry, and it was nothing I had ever desired to engage in and certainly nothing I would lead other women to participate in. So what was I to do? I did what any new mom and young pastor's wife would do: I cried! My tears led me to cry out to the Lord and lean on Him for guidance and strategy. It seems that a place of desperation accompanied with a lack of man-made form and ideology became the birthing ground for God ideas and strategy. During this season of my life God began to birth God-sized dreams and vision of His kingdom for women, and I began to run full force toward the direction of heaven.

We started with an annual women's retreat. It eventually morphed into a conference and now is the Women of Fire conference we hold every year in August. Only fourteen women attended that first retreat, and now we see women from all over the world fill our sanctuary to capacity for a gathering where we break all rules of tradition and truly seek His face and experience His glory.

It all started, however, with a yes. It started with surrender. I will never forget when the Lord asked me to surrender. It was at one of the first few women's retreats I had ever hosted. I had just finished speaking to the ladies, and we were having a simple time of prayer. We were all spread out over a cabin gathering room just crying out to God, and in that time of prayer I experienced one of the few open visions I have ever had in my life.

For a moment I wasn't at the retreat on the cabin floor. For just a moment the Lord took me somewhere else. As I opened my eyes from prayer, I didn't see the planks of hard wood anymore, but I saw a pathway of dirt and sand, like an unpaved road. I could see my feet moving, and as each foot moved into the range of my eyesight, I could see my feet had sandals on them. They were simple leather sewn sandals. The sun was hot, and the vision was so real I could feel it. "Where are we going?" I asked the Lord in my heart. I got no response, so I just kept walking. After a few moments of travel I saw before me stone steps. It was so strange, but my visual perspective from the dream was limited to the steps my feet would take. In other words, I could only see one step at a time. My scope could not take in the whole scene at once. That is very significant to what the Lord was trying to tell me on this journey. I am a big-picture person, but the Lord was choosing to limit my vision and perspective to one step at a time. Had I seen the whole picture, I may have stopped walking forward and ran in the other direction! I was just moving forward at His leading, with no clue to where I was going.

As I came to the stone steps, my feet stopped moving forward, and I stood in a moment of awkward silence. Then the Lord finally spoke to me. "Put him down," the Lord said, "and leave him here with me." In one flood of intense emotions what had been hidden from my understanding was now revealed. This journey that was so mysterious suddenly unfolded before me. I was standing at the entrance of the temple. It was as if I were standing as Hannah, but it was Jeremiah He was asking for rather than Samuel. He wanted me to take him to the temple and leave him there. Never had this Bible story been so real to me; I felt I was living out 1 Samuel 1, and I could feel Hannah's heart for the first time. I realized in that moment the great sacrifice she made in giving her young son to the Lord and how heart-wrenching that act of obedience must have been. When she placed her son in Eli's arms and then turned to walk away, there wasn't a car to hop into and drive away to drown out the cries of her baby. Just as I had to walk slowly to the temple, I realized that I would have to turn and intentionally walk away, thinking every step about what I had just done, hearing the voice of my little one the entire time.

I didn't just cry. I ugly cried. I asked the Lord why. He said, "I have need of you, and I have need of him. You can clothe him, but you can't control him."

TRUSTING GOD

Somehow I understood in that moment what the Lord meant. Although I would later study the story to understand the depth of what He was saying to me, I knew I had been trying to control my son. My identity was wrapped up in being his mother, and I was obsessed with raising him perfectly. I had my own dreams for him and my own plans. I didn't let him breathe without my knowing it. He didn't even go to the nursery or Sunday school at church because I kept him continually by my side. None of this was evil, but it was definitely getting in God's way. God gave him to me for me to be a steward of his life, not to be his god or to determine his future. I had to release him, even if it seemed he was too young and even if it hurt. Hannah must have felt pain; she may have even thought at times that what she was doing was crazy. I am sure the other mothers talked about her as if she were a terrible mom who just abandoned her son. But God never asked her to abandon him. He just asked her to release Samuel to Him, just out of the reach of her control.

Hannah's moment of release was an act of worship. As you read the first chapter of 1 Samuel, you'll see she brought an offering of worship when she released her son. She was careful with her words in saying that she "lent him to the Lord," not necessarily Eli (1 Sam. 1:28, ESV). She was giving him to God, not a man, and to her the release was an act of worship. Just as Abraham's willingness to sacrifice Isaac was an act of worship to God, so is the symbolic release of our children to Him. It is a pleasing sign of surrender of all that is valuable to us. It is the withholding of such sacrifice that is displeasing to the Lord and shows a lack of surrender and trust. In the story of Cain and Abel, Cain offered a sacrifice of convenience and less worth than that of Abel. Abel's was a sacrifice of obedience and one of life (Gen. 4:3–5; Heb. 11:4). What you put on the altar before the Lord, Mom, determines how much of a Lord He is in your life. Do you trust Him with what is most valuable to you?

Children are not a hindrance to your life and future; they are not in the way. Your destinies are intricately connected in this moment of surrender; your futures are intertwined.

I had no idea what God was about to ask me to do with my life, and I am still seeing God's plans for my son Jeremiah unfold. It was a lesson in release that up until that point I was unwilling to participate in. Sure, I had dedicated my son in church, but I had not truly given him to the Lord. I still held on very tightly and would have squeezed the life right out of both of us. God was asking me to loosen the grip and to trust Him with the son He created. God still needed me to be Jeremiah's mom, but God did not need me to be his lord. This is what every kingdom-minded mother has to learn in her journey, from the beginning to now. From Eve to Mary to Elizabeth, they all had to release control and realize that they were not the destiny makers for their children. They were merely the stewards of God's plan. God required them to walk in radical obedience to His will and not their own, even when it hurt.

What does release look like? It means just what God spoke to me: you clothe, but you don't control; you cover and equip, but you do not steer the ship. Children need covering, protection, and training, but far too many mothers have released that assignment to teachers, babysitters, or other family members. All of those individuals are at times necessary in the process of growth and development, but none of them take the place or carry the God-given responsibility of the parents, whether natural or adopted. Our moms today are saturated with options that are convenient and make life and parenting easier, but they are certainly not always what is best in the end. From eating choices to video games and peer relationships, we have traded godly parenting for convenience and ease. The sad thing is that our children suffer the most for it. God was not giving me a pass card to dump Jeremiah on someone else. He was not asking me to shift the responsibility to the church or the school or a nanny while I accomplished my own calling and goals. In fact, that could not be further from the truth. My presence in Jeremiah's life did not hinder his future any more than his presence in my life hindered my destiny. Children are not a hindrance to your life and future, Mom; they are not in the way. Instead, both of your destinies are intricately connected in this moment of surrender; your futures are intertwined. Jeremiah is a part of my future, and I am a part of his, both of us being anointed for the assignment ahead. God was changing my parenting style from ownership to stewardship.

STEWARDSHIP VERSUS OWNERSHIP

Ownership is the right of possession; it is based in entitlement. Ownership is saying, "It is mine, and I have the right to own it or take possession." Although the court of law would say this is true of my son, the kingdom of God has a different concept. Stewardship is management instead of ownership. A steward is a person who acts as a surrogate on behalf of another; a steward manages what someone else owns. Like a surrogate mother, a steward takes care of what is not her own as if it actually is her own. Her relevance and value as a steward is based on her ability to take excellent care of what is not actually hers. Jesus told the parable of the good and wicked stewards in Matthew 25:14–30, and he referred to the same concept in Luke 16:11. The wicked steward hid the coin he had been given by the master, and it did not yield any increase. The good steward invested his coin and was rewarded for the increase that came as a result. If we liken this to mothers and their children, you will see that release is what brings increase, not hoarding and hiding.

Not only must a steward be able to take care of what has been entrusted to her as if it were her own, but the steward must also champion release. Stewards must be willing to relinquish rights to the true owner when the moment comes.

Despite the fact that a surrogate mother may endure the hardships of pregnancy and labor, and she may even develop a maternal bond, she must release the baby to the parents at birth. That is the moment that release is demanded. This may seem unfair, but it was the agreement when she was given the opportunity to carry the baby. A kingdom mother understands her role is to be a steward and not an owner. I was just a steward, and the true Father and creator of Jeremiah was asking for His rights to him.

I did it. I participated in the most impactful moment of worship I had experienced in my life up until that point. Through blinding tears and unspeakable emotions I put Jeremiah on the temple steps that day. I turned and walked away, at least in the spirit, and said good-bye to controlling his life. I gave him to God that day and surrendered my sole identity as his mother. We both surrendered that day, and life has never been the same. Something shifted; destiny was unlocked in both of us in that moment, and it continues to play out in our lives. Never underestimate the power of one moment of obedience! To this day, in every decision we make about all four of our children's futures, God reminds me of that critical moment of surrender. In times of decision making, I will often hear the Holy Spirit whisper, "Clothe them; don't control them." I still have to pass the test of surrender; it's an ongoing process. I passed on that day, but with four children, it would not be my last encounter of that magnitude.

I challenge you, Mom, to have the mind-set of a steward and not an owner. As our days on this earth grow shorter and we see the unveiling of the kingdom of God among us and the approach of His return, God is beckoning for a prophetic remnant. He has designed to anoint and empower our

sons and daughters to be signs and wonders to their generation. Their time is now, not in the future, and He is looking
for more Hannahs to release their babies to His will and
plan. He is looking for moms to give it all in the highest
form of worship. One Samuel changed an entire nation. He
turned the tide and broke the cycle of religious corruption.
One mother's act of surrender saved not only her but also
God's people. What if Hannah had not obeyed? An entire
nation would have suffered. How can you, Mom, afford not
to obey also? How can you withhold what God has
freely given?

Today we make a declaration of surrender to You,
Father. We as mothers relinquish control. What
You have entrusted to us we surrender freely
back to You, and we step into the position of
steward instead of owner. We declare that our
hands will cover and not control the destiny of
our sons and daughters. We will faithfully clothe
them in the promises of God in Your Word and
establish a barrier between our seed and the
influence of the enemy. We worship You by
our surrender and trust You as the navigator of
their future. ❖

Chapter Ten
MASTERING RELEASE

A S MOTHERS WE must master the season of release. We must prepare ourselves for it because we are not the ones who determine when it arrives. Release is commanded when the Lord determines the time is right and the arrow is needed.

SURPRISED BY A SEASON OF RELEASE

I personally understand what it's like to face a season of release for which you're not quite prepared. Throughout my children's growth and development I have always kept them close and remained extremely involved in every area of their lives. Their education has been no exception. Every year Kevin and I try to remain open to how the Lord will lead, and every year He faithfully directs our decisions. We learned early not to be married to the decision of one season because seasons change. The educational needs of our children can change over time, and what worked one season is not always sufficient for the next. We have learned to move with the cloud and trust the leading of the Spirit. For some seasons we homeschooled, and for some we placed our children in a private Christian school. There was even one short season that we placed our children in public school. Regardless of the season I was involved, and I was sure their environment was conducive for their growth and development and that their spiritual lives were nurtured.

As my boys approached the transition to middle school, Jeremiah began to express a desire to attend a very prestigious all-boys boarding school in our city. At the time we lived quite a drive away from the school; it was so far off mine and Kevin's radar that we dismissed Jeremiah's suggestion every time he expressed it. It is a great school, but it definitely is not a Christian school. Boys from all over the nation and the world attended there, and with that they brought in their own religions and philosophies of life, most of which were very different from how we had raised our boys. Never did I think that God would actually design this for a season of my boys' lives.

About the same time that this desire began in Jeremiah, God began to open doors for our church to expand to an inner-city location as a second campus. I will never forget the day Kevin drove our family to see the potential church building and the Holy Spirit arrested me as we drove right past the school Jeremiah had been talking about on our way. In fact, our new church building was less than a mile from the school. What I felt in my spirit that day made me take Jeremiah's suggestions much more seriously. I began to realize that God was shifting our influence to that community, and He had already begun to draw my son's heart there. It was already the spring of his fifth-grade year. We were homeschooling at the time, and my first excuse before the Lord was that there was no way the school had vacancies. It began recruitment in the fall and was known for having waiting lists for enrollment. Its admissions process was meant to be very exclusive. After a few days of the Holy Spirit prompting me, I decided to call and at least eliminate the possibility. To my surprise, and the surprise of the admissions director I spoke to, a spot had just become available. A student who had been accepted had dropped out! My heart began to race. Could God have opened this spot for my son?

Then my second excuse before the Lord arose. There was no way we could afford the tuition of this school. I never expected the school to ask us to stop by the admissions office to officially apply! What was I doing? Yet the Holy Spirit kept prompting me to move forward, even though I did not fully understand. Through the process of application, we discovered our son qualified for a scholarship. What I never thought we could afford now became possible for us! Kevin and I began to recognize the favor of God operating on behalf of our son and knew we had to take this before the Lord in prayer. Neither of us had desired this for either of our boys. We were very unsettled and apprehensive about the carnal environment we would be planting our son in if he were to attend. It was the opposite of everything we had valued about our educational choices up until that point.

RELEASING MOSES

In a season of fasting and prayer before the Lord, God faithfully spoke to me through the story of a mother in the Bible named Jochebed. You may not know her by name, but she is the mother of Moses in the Book of Exodus.

Jochebed and her husband were a devoted Jewish couple trying to raise their family during the difficult time of Egyptian bondage. They were slaves, and so their children were born slaves. As if their bondage were not enough, Jochebed birthed a baby boy during the horrific season in Egyptian history when Pharaoh was murdering thousands of Hebrew baby boys (Exod. 1:13–14, 22). Pharaoh saw that the children of Israel were growing mighty in number, and he was afraid. He determined to cripple them by killing all the baby boys. He was not nearly as concerned with the present generation as he was with the rising generation. The enemy still has the same mind-set in our world today. He is after our babies—our future and our inheritance. I believe Satan himself influenced Pharaoh to kill the baby boys of the Hebrews because Satan was after the one whom God had anointed to deliver His people. He was after Moses. We see this same pattern today as the enemy has unleashed a ruthless assignment to destroy the children of the kingdom in this hour. Abortion alone has murdered countless potential prophetic voices to our world today. There is a reason Satan hates our children—he sees their potential to overthrow his kingdom. He knows we are more and mightier than him, just as Pharaoh came to that knowledge.

Jochebed saw something in Moses from the moment she laid eyes on him. The Word says she saw he was a "beautiful child," meaning valuable, rich, and pleasant (Exod. 2:2).[1] This moment was more than a mother falling in love with her newborn baby. She saw something about him in the spirit and knew he must be preserved for great purpose. As kingdom mothers we must have this type of vision. We cannot be limited to the exterior appearance of our children. Instead, we must see with spiritual vision their value and potential in the kingdom. What Jochebed saw led her to make extreme decisions concerning her son's care, and what we see in our son will determine the decisions we make with his future also.

Jochebed's first strategy to protect her son and the purpose he was to fulfill was to hide him (Exod. 2:2). She literally kept him from the view of the enemy and covered him continually. This was what was safest and best for the first season of his life, and we can see this same parallel in the care of our own children. There is a season for hiding, for holding them close, and for keeping them near. Even Hannah was allowed to keep Samuel until he was weaned before she presented him at the temple (1 Sam. 1:22). This is what comes naturally to us as mothers: we see the need to guard our children from harm, and that is a God-given instinct.

However, the story of Exodus lets us know that a point in time came that the Word tells us Jochebed could "no longer hide him" (Exod. 2:3). She could not let what had been the best choice for one season become a danger to him the next. The season changed and along with it her role as protector in his life. She had to find a new strategy to guard the value and potential she saw in him. She had to release him to save him.

PREPARING FOR RELEASE

Pharaoh has ordered that all boys be thrown into the Nile River to drown (Exod. 1:22). How horrible a sight it must have been to see those innocent babies being overcome by the water of the river! And how ironic that the river is the place where Jochebed was led to take Moses. That definitely seems like a move in the wrong direction. She should be taking him far away from the danger, not leading him to it. However, the river was where Moses would find his destiny and purpose. It was not his enemy, even though it carried potential danger. Whether or not the river would be an aid to his destiny or a hazard to his survival would be determined by how he would be released into its waters. To me, the river in this story can symbolize life. Life itself is full of hazards and dangers to our children. Our first tendency can be to run from it. However, the journey of life is a necessary pathway for our children to find purpose and destiny. Jochebed could not keep Moses from the river forever, and we cannot keep our children from the journey of life in this sin-fallen world, either. Avoidance is not an option. It all comes down to how we equip them for release into its turbulent waters.

So many little boys before Moses had drowned in the Nile River. They were tossed into its current with no covering, no protection, no preparation, and no care. They were not ready to face it on their own. They were released too early and without the tools for survival. They were overtaken by its waters. We can see the parallel in the spirit realm. We cannot toss our children to the current of life before they are ready. They cannot skip the season of hiding and guarding and nurturing. It is necessary for their survival. And even when that season ends and the river of life is inevitable, we must equip them for their journey. What separated Moses from the other Hebrew boys in the Nile was something called "an ark" (Exod. 2:3, KJV). The same word was used to describe the covering that protected Noah in the flood and preserved him when the world around him was perishing. As we begin to slowly release our children into life without our constant covering and supervision—in school, with friends, or at church—we must also equip them with an ark that will keep them despite the potential danger in the waters.

Jochebed acquired a basket that was made of bulrush (Exod. 2:3). The material it was constructed of was what must have drawn her to it. Bulrush actually grows in the waters of the Nile River. It comes from the Hebrew word *gome*, meaning "to absorb," because it absorbs air in its pours.[2] This makes bulrush very buoyant. Jochebed literally took something from where Moses was going in order to equip him with something that had experience in the river. It could float on top of what other plants sink in.[3]

As we equip our children for a moment of release, we must follow this same concept. We have to give them the tools of wisdom and experience gathered from where they are going so they have something to float in when they face life. Their first contact with the river cannot be at release; as Jochebed did, we must bring pieces of the river to them so that in the spirit we give them buoyance when the waters rage. Experience and wisdom imparted to our children from our own lives and from the lives of others create a basket they can float in when they find themselves in the river. By mentoring our children for real-life circumstances, we give them the opportunity to float and not sink. Don't just shield them from life but train them on how to encounter it.

After Jochebed got a bulrush basket, she began to coat it "with slime and with pitch" (Exod. 2:3, KJV). Yuck! It even sounds gross. Can you imagine what that did to that beautiful basket? Jochebed knew the materials of slime and pitch all too well. Slime was a mud substance that was used in the brick-making process of Egypt. The pitch was a tar-like substance that was primarily used for embalming the dead. These two materials represented the life of the Hebrew slaves of Egypt. They daily spent their lives and energy making pyramids of bricks for Pharaoh, and they were daily surrounded by death. Not only did Jochebed reach forward into the river of Moses's future and pull out choice materials to help him float, but she also reached back into where he had been in his family's history of slavery and coated the beautiful basket in the reality of his past. It wasn't pretty, but it was necessary. In order for Moses to survive the river and find his destiny, the ugly roots of his past were necessary reminders. The testimony of his parents' slavery would be key in his future. He had to remember where he came from. The slime and pitch waterproofed that little ark so that he could be in the water without the water touching him. His roots kept him from taking the river in his boat! Our children too need to be grounded in where they have come from—not as a weight, but as a testimony to the power of God. Whether it is beautiful or whether it is like pitch and slime, the roots you as a mother have provided for your children will allow them to be in the world but keep the world from being in them.

Not only were the pitch and slime reminders of his roots, they were also Jochebed's way of taking what was intended to harm Moses and using it for his good. Does that not bring a familiar scripture to mind? Genesis 50:20 speaks of this. If the Nile had not taken Moses, the slavery of Egypt would have been his fate. The same material that symbolized his harm was used by his mother and by God to spare his life! The enemy's weapons backfired!

TRUSTING GOD IN THE RELEASING

Once Jochebed had properly prepared Moses, she released him into the Nile. At that point all she could do was trust God and trust the ark her hands had made. She let him go into the river, and it became a pathway to his purpose. The area in which she left Moses was near the area where the daughter of Pharaoh bathed. It was a divine setup. As soon as Pharaoh's daughter saw the baby boy in the basket, she had compassion on him and took him into her arms and into her home (Exod. 2:6–10). She had no idea that the little innocent baby she drew out of the water would be the demise of the entire kingdom of Egypt. Jochebed had literally planted a bomb in the enemy's territory! A secret weapon was released in Pharaoh's house that day, and it was all because of the obedience of a little Hebrew mother.

Remember that what you release to the Lord will return to you. What you sow into His hands will always return with increase. Because of Jochebed's obedience God abundantly rewarded her. God set her up through her daughter Miriam to become the wet nurse of her own son for Pharaoh's daughter (Exod. 2:7–8). She went from having to hide her son and her connection

If I just kept building an ark for them, they would float and not sink.

to him to being paid by the enemy to care for him! She no longer had to live in fear, but she could openly nurture her son again. During this time with Moses, Jochebed was able to influence his life without the fear of his death, and her impact stayed with him. In fact, what she poured into him in those few years kept him faithful to his purpose even after a lifetime in the influence of Egypt. And his training in Egypt gave him the knowledge and influence to later lead God's people in the Exodus from their slavery.

PREPARING AND RELEASING JEREMIAH

This is the word God gave to me as I prayed about my son attending this new school. It was time for a new level of release. God said it was time to plant a bomb in the enemy's territory. He told me not to run from the waters, but that Jeremiah and Isaiah were equipped to use the current as a pathway to destiny. They needed the education of Egypt for the purpose of their futures, whatever they may hold. If I just kept building an ark for them, they would float and not sink; they would be in the river but not become like it.

That day I surrendered Jeremiah to the river, and Isaiah would soon follow. However, I did not release them without the proper tools and equipment to succeed. They were tucked inside an ark that could handle the current. It doesn't mean that water didn't try to get in at times, but their roots kept them waterproof. They began to bear fruit in a place I knew many others had not survived. They did not just survive, but they thrived in the river.

Ironically the Lord let us know it would be a season. Just as Moses did not remain in Egypt forever, so our sons would not stay in this school forever. We saw this play out as they completed their middle school years and entered high school. But the decision to release Jeremiah to this new environment was the divine will of the Lord, and He confirmed it all the way. They walked in their own anointing and favor and impacted those they came in contact with daily. The river took them toward their destiny.

I declare over you, Mom, the vision of Jochebed. I pray you see your children with the eyes of the Spirit and not just natural vision. I pray that what you see will cause you to radically obey with every decision of their future. May God give you the grace to hide them when needed and the grace to release them when commanded. I pray for strategy for constructing an ark and intentionality in preparing for release into the river of life. I declare your children will float and not sink and will find destiny in the river. May they overcome what others have been overcome by, and may they be living, breathing bombs in the enemy's territory! ❖

Chapter Eleven
CLOTHE THEM;
DON'T CONTROL THEM

>>>>•————————————•

A S KINGDOM MOTHERS we must adopt the identity of steward and not owner when it comes to the spiritual development and deployment of our children. In the story of Samuel and Hannah we see that Hannah's obedience to her promise to God led her to the steps of the temple to do something that most mothers never could have done: she took her baby boy there and left him in the daily care of a corrupt priest. However, Hannah's connection with Samuel was not severed, and her influence on his life and development did not end on the day she left him at the temple. There was continued influence, relationship, and communication about his purpose in the location he was assigned. I don't believe for one moment that Samuel was ever in the dark about why his mother left him or what his purpose was at the temple. His understanding obviously grew as he matured and experienced God, but Samuel did not live in an identity crisis. He was groomed from birth for his service to the Lord and embraced it fully. The influence of his mother and her prayers and his encounter with the presence of God (1 Sam. 3) kept him from following the corrupt pattern set before him in Eli's sons.

CLOTHING YOUR CHILD FROM SELF-DOUBT

The Word says that Samuel wore a linen ephod (1 Sam. 2:18). This was a typical priestly garment that was worn in the service at the temple. The Word does not clearly state if Eli gave Samuel this, but it can be assumed that he dressed him for his duties. In addition to the ephod, there was a powerful garment of influence made for Samuel by his mother every year (1 Sam. 2:19). It was an outer garment or cloak, and the original word in this passage could even be interpreted as an ephod[1] that she brought every time she came for her yearly act of worship. It was not a one-time gift, but it was something she did annually and something she tailored to fit his growth. He wore it every day, and it was a tangible message from his mother, even when she was not with him.

Garments have always represented identity, especially in this context. In Bible times individuals could be identified simply by what they wore. This was true especially in religious circles. We read of the different garments in the service of the priesthood (Exod. 39:41). We even read of the robes that identified the king (1 Kings 22:10), the garments that signified the virginity of the king's daughters (2 Sam. 13:18), the outer mantle of the prophets such as Elijah (2 Kings 2:13), and the torn clothing that a person with leprosy was forced to wear, according to Leviticus 13:45. Even beggars wore an identifying garment, as we see in the story of blind Bartimaeus (Mark 10:50). Garments made unspoken statements of an individual's status and identity. The type of coat Hannah made for Samuel was an outer garment that would show his true identity, even as a child.

The coat she made was the Hebrew word $m^{e c}\hat{\imath}yl$. This meant it was not just any ordinary garment, but one worn by men of rank, kings' daughters, or even the high priest himself.[2]

Whereas Eli may have dressed him in a simple linen ephod as he ministered or served in the temple, Hannah took his identity to the next level by dressing him in a garment that made a statement of his rank and value. She saw what Eli did not see or refused to see. Eli's perspective of Samuel was limited to what he was currently capable of producing. However, his mother saw beyond the present day to his future capacity. She saw what he was capable of becoming. He was not just any priest; he was of high rank, royalty, and could even be the high priest. Samuel was not left to discover his own identity, and his identity was not left to be defined by a corrupt priest or wicked brothers. His mother's garment shielded him from what anyone else would want him to be, and it shielded him from the labels of man's false identity. Even on days when he may have doubted himself, it would have been the continual message of his mother's garment that reminded him of the word of the Lord over his life.

The garment Samuel wore not only established rank and position, but it also was a tangible representation of the favor of God upon his life. Similarly Joseph's coat of many colors demonstrated the favor of his earthly father as well as of the heavenly Father upon his life (Gen. 37:3). From being thrown into a pit and left for dead, to being falsely accused in the house of Potiphar, to imprisonment, the favor and anointing upon Joseph's life always caused him to rise above his circumstances. (See Genesis 37–45.) The enemy could not keep him down or destroy his purpose. In spite of all those circumstances, the favor on his life still elevated him to the palace where the message of his coat came to fulfillment. The garment that his father clothed him with could not be tarnished by his brothers or even by Pharaoh himself. Even

THE WARRIOR WE CALL MOM

when the actual coat was taken and destroyed, its message remained with Joseph.

This is the role of a kingdom-minded parent, to carefully stitch a covering of identity that the world cannot take away or tarnish. Hannah covered Samuel; she did not control him. She covered him not with her physical hands or strength, but with an identity that came straight from the mouth of God that she, in turn, established by the words of her mouth. This is what our children need in this hour and in the darkness that they will face; they need a covering. Your presence as their parent cannot always protect and keep them, but their identity in Christ will. It will keep them from compromise and corruption, and it will preserve them in the face of adversity. Like in a garment, they need to intentionally dress themselves in their identity as sons and daughters of God every day.

Yet another example of this is in the story of the three Hebrew boys. Their mothers could not keep them from captivity in Babylon. In fact, they were placed right in the heart of leadership of such a wicked kingdom, in the care and influence of the king. Babylon wanted them because of their favor and anointing, just as the world will seek the favor and anointing of our children. It desires to use them for its own selfish purposes. Even though their mothers could not control their placement and keep them out of Babylon, those women obviously instilled an identity in their sons that kept Babylon out of them. Those Hebrew boys never bowed to the idolatry of the culture, and they never tried to blend in with Babylonians because they were secure in who they already were. (See Daniel 3:8–18.)

Hannah did not control Samuel's destiny, but she actively clothed him. When her presence was not possible, her influence was undeniable. When she could not keep corruption

138

and the attacks of the enemy from him, the identity she had carefully constructed for him, year after year, covered him. Moms, we cannot keep our children from the world, and they are not meant to be hidden. They are to be in the world but not of it, and how you cover them can be what sets them apart.

My children still make fun of me for the way I bundle them up in cold weather. There have been many household jokes about the time it takes for my children to get dressed to go play in the snow. My heart desires to simply keep them warm and dry while they play in the freezing weather. I don't want to keep them from the snow; I just want to protect them in it. This is what we can do for our children as we send them out into life. We should not think the answer lies in keeping them locked in our homes for the rest of their lives! Just as snow gear that you bundle them in shields them from the elements, so the identity you declare and foster over them shields them and allows them to thrive in conditions that would normally be destructive. This is the power of the garment you construct for your children, and this is the will of the Lord for their lives.

> *We cannot keep our children from the world, and they are not meant to be hidden.... How you cover them can be what sets them apart.*

Because of the anointing and favor upon them as sons and daughters of God, they should thrive regardless of the environment they are deployed to in their future.

GODLY WORDS RELEASE GODLY FAVOR

Shaping identity is hard work, and it is shaped in more than just one moment. It is very similar to the process of stitching together a garment. The value of a garment comes from the material from which it is made and the time that is invested in making it. A great deal of time and effort are made for one single garment, especially if it is designed for one particular individual. As a mother you are not making a garment that is meant to be mass-produced to fit all the children in your home equally. Each child gets a new, tailor-made garment.

As a mother of four children, I have found that hand-me-downs are inevitable. The younger siblings in our home are accustomed to wearing last season's garments without complaining. However, the excitement they display when they receive new clothes of their own is incredible to see! They appreciate them so much more. My youngest daughter especially likes monogrammed clothing. Once her name or initials are on something, she knows it is only hers. It allows for a strong sense of ownership she does not carry for hand-me-downs. She takes greater care of the clothing that is brand-new or marked with her initials. It is hers, and she is proud of it!

Shaping identity is hard work, and it is shaped in more than just one moment.... It happens stitch by stitch and day by day.

This is how the calling and purpose of our children's lives should be presented to them. Purpose is not a hand-me-down destiny inherited from parents, grandparents, or older siblings. It is not a garment that others can wear the same way. Their purpose is a garment that has been tailor-made for them alone. It may have similar colors and material as the garments that other members of the family wear, but it is uniquely theirs. It is not happenstance; their purpose is designed specifically for them, with their names on the labels. This will cause your children to view their future and purpose with greater care and ownership. As long as they think their purpose can be filled by someone else or that their destiny is up for grabs, they may not step up to the plate of responsibility.

The making of a secure identity, as with a tailor-made garment, does not happen overnight. It happens stitch by stitch and day by day, with every word and action enforcing and creating a covering. We as moms must continually cut away excess, stitch together pieces, and measure material to fit their stage of development, making every stitch with great thought and purpose. Words and actions work together to produce such a garment in the Spirit, but words have a greater impact on identity. The greatest weapon you have as a child of God is the ability to speak words. This powerful weapon can be used for the kingdom or by the enemy. Words in prayer, words in declaration, and even words in conversation form the atmosphere and covering of your family and contain a power that cannot always be seen in the natural moment of release.

The heavens and the earth were created by words, and in our God-given nature our words have creative power. Proverbs 18:21 lets us know that our words create either life or death. And so it is over our children. It is words, prayers, and blessings declared over them that serve as a large part of their identity formation. The weapon of declaration and blessing should be used regularly in our homes. Far too often our homes are filled with negative confessions and slander, tearing down one another. These negative declarations tear their identity like tearing a garment. However, it is the intent of God to establish an atmosphere of blessing in the home on a regular basis. Just as the heavens were established by the word of the Lord, so your home can be established by the Word.

When the earth was formed, a day called the Sabbath was established. It was a day set aside as holy before the Lord.

To this day the Jewish people still hold this day as holy and have many traditions and rituals surrounding Shabbat, or the Sabbath. Every Friday evening, the beginning of the Sabbath, they practice the power of blessing. As Sabbath dinner begins, a candle is lit, and the father places his hands upon the head of each of his children and releases a spoken blessing over them. This weekly practice shapes identity and releases the favor of God. The words we speak either create a tapestry of life in our homes and children, or they weave a garment of death and destruction. What you verbally affirm over your children will flourish, whether it be negative attributes or positive ones. We must train ourselves as parents to release life by declaring blessings into our homes, words that our children can hear themselves. We are responsible for harnessing and sharpening the weapons of our tongues as parents. Develop a daily practice of positive declaration by writing your own blessing and speaking it over your children on a regular basis. We do this every night at bedtime in the Wallace house. The last voice our children hear is of one of their parents quoting the blessings of God's Word over them.

I believe a daily declaration of the Word of God to your children will weave a garment over them that the enemy cannot penetrate. Don't agree with the identity the enemy would cover them with, but combat it with the truth of God's Word. When they fail in honesty or integrity, don't attach a label of unrighteous behavior to them. Instead, speak life and truth over them even in the midst of their struggles. Speak over them what they can be and will be according to God's Word, even when they have yet to become it. Doing so is planting seeds into the soil of their hearts that will produce fruit in due season. And I believe a good harvest can overtake any bad one.

SHAPING THROUGH GODLY DISCIPLINE

Another strategic way to shape a spiritual garment of identity for your child is in daily discipline and decision making. The purpose of discipline is not to achieve control but to align us with destiny. Decisions either align us toward or move us further from purpose. Standards and rules should be in place to shape identity and give purpose behind actions. Don't just tell your children to do something or not to do something; help them understand why. They don't have to agree, but they should be given the opportunity to begin to understand. They should couple actions with consequences, whether negative or positive. Let them know that negative or rebellious behavior doesn't line up with who they are in Christ and will only lead them away from their destiny and potential, causing them to miss the mark. Again, don't agree with negative behavior and sew it into their garment. Discipline should center around molding your children to their destiny and toward obedience to the Lord. The focus should be their future and not their temporal comfort or pleasure.

Every major life decision should be centered around identity and destiny. From schooling to athletics to peers, help your children steer these decisions through the filter of who God has created them to be. As they grow older, you should even help them steer through how their own desires can be in conflict with the plans of God. Time is more valuable than gold, so if it consumes their time, it should be weighed before the Lord. Be careful not to let the pressure of culture or society begin to steer their schedule, only the expectations of the Father. Matthew 11:30 assures us that His burden is easy and His yoke is light. This can be reflected in every aspect of your children's lives, even their daily schedules. The demands placed upon young people in our culture today are off balance because the demands align their daily lives to the world's expectation and choke out precious time that should be spent in His presence. Business does not always equal fruitfulness and is more often than not a fruit killer. This is why we have so many young people who are busy, stressed, burned-out, and directionless. They are busier now than they have ever been, yet they are more disconnected from kingdom purposes. Their lives are so consumed by activities that time spent hearing from God and being shaped by Him falls to the wayside. They are not living life through the filter of God identity, but instead through the filter of societal pressure and expectations. We as moms are caught right in the middle of the struggle, chauffeuring them to their own destruction. Our families are far too stretched, everyone going in his own direction, and we have lost our family synergy centered around fellowship together with Him. Let our schedules reflect God's purposes, and don't invest time and money in worldly goals that will never bear fruit. As parents we have to ask ourselves a question that my husband felt the Spirit of the Lord prompted him to ask himself: "Am I raising my children to be famous, or raising them so He (Christ) can be famous through them?"

DON'T GET STUCK IN YESTERDAY'S IDENTITY

Just as natural garments have to grow and expand with the growth and maturity of our children, so it is in the Spirit. Destiny unfolds and is further revealed as maturity occurs. You can't get stuck in yesterday's garment or be limited in your understanding to just a single moment or season in time. What is fulfilling purpose in one season of your child's life may not be what God has assigned him to do in the next.

It may merely be a prepping season. If my son wore the same shoes for five years in a row, the shoes would become insufficient over time. In fact, because the shoes would have no capacity to grow with my son, what

> *Every major life decision should be centered around identity and destiny.*

covered him in one season would become a restriction in the next. The limited capacity of the shoes would become a hindrance to his mobility and even restrict and deform his growth! Just like shoes or seasonal garments, your understanding of your child's identity and purpose must grow and mature as your child does. Even Hannah brought a new garment every year as Samuel grew (1 Sam. 2:19). Give them some growing room, and keep a continual ear to heaven to hear the Lord's heart for each season.

TRAIN UP A CHILD...

Shaping our children for their God purpose begins with our own ability to hear and obey God. According to 1 Samuel 1:11, Hannah called Samuel to the Nazarite vow from birth. She made the vow that a razor would never touch his head and began to train him for a lifestyle he did not have the ability or maturity to choose on his own. She groomed him for the temple, even though Eli had yet to make such mandates on his life. Similarly Samson's mother in the Book of Judges chose a lifestyle for Samson that was not his own decision to make. But there came a day in Samuel's life when he no longer had to be dressed by someone else. He could wake up and dress himself as he came to the age of adulthood. There came a season in his life when either he could embrace what his life had conditioned him for, accept his mother's

Nazarite declaration over him, and follow the plan of God for his life, or he could refuse it. He could throw down his mother's coat and turn in his ephod and find his own way in life. The truth is we can train our children to follow God, but we cannot make them follow God. We may make the garment, but there comes a season in their maturity that they must choose to put it on themselves.

There are two particular Bible stories that come to mind that demonstrate how children of promise may still waver from the values they were clothed with, at least for a season. In the life of Samson in the Book of Judges we see that he willfully went in a direction in which God and his parents directed him not to go. For a season he experienced the pain and heartache of his choices because they resulted in his becoming a prisoner to the Philistines. However, his hair did grow back, and at the end of his life he turned back to his true God purpose and won a great victory against the enemies of God's people. It took a season of defeat to help him realign to a place of victory. (See Judges 13–16.)

We also see in the story of the prodigal son in Luke 15 how one son remained in his father's house while the other took his inheritance and began to live his life in a manner that was contrary to his upbringing. His poor life

Your understanding of your child's identity and purpose must grow and mature as your child does.

choices left him in rags instead of the beautiful garments his parents had clothed him in. However, the Word says he came to himself in the midst of the pigpen. Something snapped within him, and he turned from his wicked ways and willfully chose to return to his father's house. From the moment his father saw him coming toward his home, he prepared a robe to re-cover him and bring him back into his rightful place of identity and purpose.

Mom, even if your daughter chooses to throw off her proper garments for a time, don't lose heart. It may take a defeat before she finds victory again. It could take a season in the pigpen before she surrenders her will to the heavenly Father. However, garments can be restored, and destiny does not have to be forfeited. The garment you are weaving for your child will endure through wavering and testing, and that purpose will remain beyond the elements of doubt and deception.

Right now I declare a grace to come upon every mother to clothe but not control the purpose and destiny of the precious life entrusted to her. Mom, may you have the discernment to hear God's voice as you daily weave a garment of identity that will protect and shield your child from the deception of the enemy. May all wayward sons and daughters come to themselves in the name of Jesus and throw off the rags of self-doubt and deception for the royal garments God has purposed for them to wear. I pray right now that we see the release of a generation that is clothed in garments that declare our children's royal positions as sons and daughters in God's kingdom. May they spend their days fulfilling purpose instead of consuming their lives with searching for purpose. ❖

Chapter Twelve
BE FIERCE, NOT AFRAID

>>>>•———————————•

THROUGHOUT THE BOOK of Judges we read of mighty leaders who judged Israel and also led it in military victory. In this list of chosen leaders we find an unconventional female judge whose name was Deborah, and she was given the title of mother over Israel. God Himself chose and anointed a mother figure to not only rule in wisdom but also lead the entire nation into battle. Not only did God anoint Deborah as judge, but He also used another unassuming female warrior to win the victory for His people. Deborah's bold leadership led to the historical victory, but it was not actually Deborah or even the mighty general Barak whose hands defeated the enemy. It was the hands of someone who lacked skilled military training and had probably never even been on the battlefield before. She probably didn't even own a sword and certainly didn't know how to use one! It was the leadership of Deborah but the hands of a young lady named Jael that won the battle that won the war!

This seemingly unarmed, untrained housewife, who was just keeping her tent while the men were at battle, stepped out in bold obedience and loyalty to the Lord and won the victory. (See Judges 4.) We must look a little more closely to this story of heroism by Jael to see that a woman who keeps her home is by no means weak or weaponless, but she is an adversary the enemy is no match for!

What I love about the story in Judges 4 is that God reveals

149

His heart and His ability to use women in places that society has declared, in times past, women cannot be effective. We first find Deborah acting as the mother to an entire nation (Judg. 5:7). She sat in her seat of authority under the palm tree and ruled with grace. Meanwhile Israel was living under the cruel oppression of King Jabin and the Canaanite people (Judg. 4:2). It must have angered Deborah's heart to see her dear children treated with such cruelty, but there came a point when the Lord and Deborah had had enough. Deborah felt the inward fight that only a mother could understand, and as soon as God gave the signal, she moved without hesitation to a position of battle. The command came from her lips for Barak to assemble his men and lead them toward the armies of Sisera, for the enemy who had once oppressed them would now be delivered into their hands (Judg. 4:6–7). Deborah never faltered in her faith in God, even though Barak responded with an answer signifying doubt in God's ability to deliver them (v. 8). Although Barak was afraid, Deborah was not! What a mighty woman of God Deborah must have been that the leader of Israel's armies would not go into battle without her! Upon Barak's invitation Deborah rode in the chariot alongside him into battle, a seat a woman would not normally sit in.

Just be ready, woman of God. We are entering a season when women will sit in places of authority and leadership that have not traditionally been open to us. There is a leadership shift happening in the kingdom, and the influence and strength of women and mothers will be needed for the victory in this hour! Because of Barak's reluctance to obey the Word of the Lord, he lost the glory of victory, and because of Deborah's faith in God the Lord declared that the victory of the battle would belong to a woman.

FIERCE, NOT FEARFUL

Who ever said women, especially mothers, are weak? The fact that God has entrusted women with the act of child-birth alone should reflect His confidence in the strength and endurance of a woman. I am convinced if my husband would have had to give birth to our babies, we would not have children! I have to laugh as I vividly remember the nurses having to attend to Kevin during the birth of our children because he either had passed out or was vomiting. He could not handle the delivery room. We as mothers, however, have been designed and created for that moment, both physically and emotionally. We were created to birth life.

We are not made to be fearful, but fierce. We are not made to be cowards, but to be helpmates. The word *helpmeet* is actually the Hebrew word *ezer*. As we discussed earlier, it is the name that God gave woman when He determined that Adam needed her;[1] in fact, God uses the word *ezer* to describe Himself. *Ezer* can be likened to a deliverer in battle, and that is a true helpmeet! Woman was created to be a war-rior alongside her man. She was created to birth and protect the seed of humanity. The enemy knows this about woman, but few women realize this about themselves.

There is nothing more intimidating or fierce than a woman whose children have been threatened. Just mess with the bear cubs of a momma bear or the little ducklings of a mother duck, and you will see; a woman who loves her chil-dren will stop at nothing to guard and protect them! There have only been a few times in my life that I have totally blown my witness as a follower of Christ and come close to ending up in jail. Those few times all had one common denomi-nator: someone messed with one of the Wallace kids. I may be only five feet tall, but there was not one sane thought in my mind when I felt the need to defend my family. Kevin has always said that I may not know karate, but I do know crazy. Remember, it is not the size of the person in the fight, but it's the size of the fight in the person. Mothers are born with a vicious drive to fight for and defend what belongs to them. The enemy knows this fact, and that is why he targets and intimidates mothers with fear and doubt. He knows the potential deadly force that will be awakened when Spirit-filled mothers take their place on the battlefield, and his strategy is to bind you with fear.

GENERATIONAL SYNERGY

In Judges 4 we see the deadly force of mothers taking their place in battle. First there is Deborah, the seasoned mother who dared to mount a chariot, a place that was unheard of for women. She has a voice that carries weight and authority. When I think of Deborah, I think of the church mothers at our own church. They have advanced past the season of physical motherhood, yet they never cease to act in the authority of motherhood. Deborah was guarding Israel as if the Israelites were her children, even though they were not hers by birth. She understood spiritual motherhood. I pray that we will see a revival of spiritual mothers in the church—mothers who will guard and protect in intercession and spiritual warfare those who are not even their natural children, spiritual mothers who will walk in wisdom and sound judgment and be a support to the community of faith around them. I pray seasoned mothers will undergird and support young mothers in need of guidance and strength. I pray for a revival of seasoned mothers who will awaken the warrior within the younger mothers. There is no retirement season in the life of a true mother. The old African proverb states, "It takes a village to raise a child." I fear that in our faith-based villages known as churches, we are missing one of the most vital parts of the tribe, and that is our seasoned warriors. It was Deborah who declared the Word of the Lord over Jael and released the blessing of God over her after her victory (Judg. 5:24). She supported and affirmed the

We are not made to be fearful, but fierce. We are not made to be cowards, but to be helpmates.

anointing upon her life. These two women shook the gates of the enemy and won a victory for the entire community. I pray for a revival of the unification of the older and younger mothers in the kingdom of God. This will produce a unified front that the kingdom of darkness cannot withstand.

In my own life and ministry to young girls who have been victims of horrific abuse and violence, I have felt the grace and anointing of spiritual motherhood. These daughters are not mine by birth, but they are young women we work to restore through our programs with The Zion Project, and they have captured my heart as a mother. I have a burden from heaven in my soul that will drive me to pray over them at the most random times. I can look into their eyes and see their potential in spite of all of their scars and baggage. I see the beauty in them when the world may see them as less than valuable, just as a mother would see beauty in her own child even if everyone else thought he or she was ugly. If all of the mothers in the world would ask for the burden of spiritual motherhood, I am convinced shortages in the realm of adoptions, foster care, and group homes would cease. I think gang violence and drug usage in our youth would decrease. If we as mothers would dare to love those who are not biologically our own, we could revolutionize our communities.

As I type this, I am watching my boys play video games with their newest cousins, two precious boys from Ethiopia, adopted by a member of our extended family. Two young boys who had been abandoned and left in hopeless situations are now excelling in school and athletics, loving Jesus, and having the gift of family. They are our family, even if we don't look the same on the outside. My son Isaiah has developed such a special bond with the boys and has cried hot tears over their stories of early childhood in the village back in Ethiopia.

The truth of the kingdom is that it took both a Deborah and a Jael to defeat the enemy. Together, and not in a spirit of criticism or competition, they delivered their nation.

It's a learning experience and global perspective for my children that will forever impact their hearts toward the world around them. They have seen firsthand the difference that can be made by supernatural love. This is an example of spiritual motherhood to a greater extreme, and I believe these boys will, in turn, impact the kingdom of God. They were rescued for a purpose. I believe the Lord will abundantly bless those who open their hearts for the abandoned and broken, and I believe that these boys can shake the nation of Ethiopia.

GOD HAS A PERSONALIZED PLAN FOR YOU

Deborah represents the spiritual mother and the woman on the front line who stands in the public eye and in the sights of the enemy. She was the leader out front, the lady preacher, the pastor's wife, the political leader, the conference speaker whom everyone could see, as she operated in the spotlight and notoriety. But there was a silent and unassuming warrior who was not on the front lines or even in the midst of the battle. No one may have even known her name. She was simply in her tent, her dwelling place. This describes so many women I come into contact with as I travel in ministry.

They live under the deception that they are ineffective in the kingdom of God around them because they are not doing something that is visible to others or recognized by their peers. They feel they are trapped in their homes doing laundry and potty-training babies, and the world is passing them by. They would never think that the focus of the battle could show up at their front door and that the deciding victory could take place in their living room. I wonder if Jael ever thought about Deborah and entertained statements such as, "I wonder what it would be like to be Deborah. I wish I could lead like Deborah. Why can't I do what Deborah does?"

This is a common source of tension in our society today, the clash between the working mom and the stay-at-home mom, the conflict between what the world deems a "successful" woman because of a salary and a title, and a woman who forfeits a paycheck and stays within the home. We can criticize both, but the truth is that both are needed. I am convinced God has a personalized plan for each of His daughters' lives. He may assign one to the workplace and one to her home. He may place one on the mission field and one in a government office and call one to homeschool. The truth of Judges 4 and the truth of the kingdom is that it took both a Deborah and a Jael to defeat the enemy. It took a woman on the front lines of battle riding in a chariot and a woman who was keeping her tent. Together, and not in a spirit of criticism or competition, they delivered their nation. Never forget, Mom, that all seasons have specific timing and an expiration date. What God has assigned for you today may change in the near future. Don't define your destiny by a season. Embrace the season you are in, and find your place and value in the kingdom wherever God positions you. What God defines as success does not center around diplomas, titles, or annual salaries. What God defines as success is a woman positioned in obedience to His leading and surrendered to His will. This type of woman can be used to win the victory with or without a sword.

Lord, I declare that a unification of generations would manifest itself in Your church in this hour. I declare that the seasoned generation will shake off a mentality of retirement and allow the passion of spiritual motherhood to consume them. I pray a mentality shift over our stay-at-home moms who may not see their kingdom significance in this season. May they awaken and see their potential within. May they shake off feelings of insignificance and discouragement. I pray grace over working mothers who carry the load of home and workplace. May they lead where You call and shake off the burdens You have not called them to carry. May they successfully follow You and still lead their homes to bear the fruit of the kingdom. I declare a rising up of Deborahs and Jaels hand in hand who will defeat the enemy for this generation! ❖

Chapter Thirteen
BREAKING GENERATIONAL CYCLES

>»»————————————•»

You might be similar to Jael today—a mom who dwells in her tent and is faithful in her own territory, seemingly unarmed and far from dangerous to your adversary. You may be looking at other women who seem to embody what society deems success, and you may feel "less than" or even wrestle feelings of failure. You may choose to believe that the battle is someone else's responsibility because you are up to your eyes in laundry. You may even be content leaving it to the men or even other moms. But this is a lie of the enemy because you, woman of God, are the secret weapon that God desires to use on the front line in this season in the kingdom. There is a battlefield shift taking place, and the war zone is the home. The battle in your house may affect the battle in the nation. Can you even imagine that something you conquer in your wartime of prayer may actually shape the future of households around you? This was the story of Jael. She fought the one battle that would win the war all by herself in her living room!

STOP SLEEPING WITH THE ENEMY

The battle for territory in the kingdom is raging in our nation and in the world. The war zone is not just limited to political arenas and government leaders. The war zone is not just confined to the church and its leaders. The enemy has dared to venture into our homes. He has targeted our families! The enemy has become so confident and brash that he has crossed the threshold of our dwelling places and has attempted to find rest, comfort, and refuge in our personal space. He wants to make our homes his command center, working to destroy the church and our nation by destroying the family unit. The fight is in your children's bedrooms. The fight is in your family room. The battle is raging around your dinner table. The enemy wants your seed and will cross all boundaries to steal and destroy. You, Mom, are the one who stands between your children and the enemy. Are you providing him asylum and safety by operating in compromise and complacency? Are you allowing family alliances with the adversary through fear or apathy?

It was an unhealthy family alliance that opened the door to the enemy in the tent of Jael. Why did Sisera boldly enter Jael's dwelling place? The Word lets us know that Jael was the wife of Heber the Kenite (Judg. 4:17). In this story the children of Israel had been sold into slavery because of their wickedness. Their slave master was Jabin (v. 2). He was the ruler of the Canaanites, who oppressed the children of God, so he was the clear enemy. Heber, Jael's husband, had an alliance of peace with Jabin. The Word

> *The enemy wants your seed and will cross all boundaries to steal and destroy.*

literally says the house (family) of Heber had peace with Jabin (v. 17). Jael's husband had made a family agreement of peace with the enemy, which brings a whole new twist to the phrase "sleeping with the enemy"! Jael's lineage literally had an unhealthy alliance with the enemy of God's people! How many of us have inherited family alliances with the enemy? How many of us have watched a grandpa, grandma, aunt, uncle, or even spouse make a deal of compromise with the devil and welcome the enemy right into our homes and our children's lives? This could be through generational demons that darken our closets, addictions, diseases, perversions, brokenness, alcoholism, divorce, homosexuality, and the list continues. How many of us have ever identified patterns of iniquity that haunt our lineage? Have you recognized the tendencies or bents toward sin and sickness from generation to generation in your family line that you may feel helpless to defend yourself against?

The Book of Isaiah says that Jesus Christ was wounded for our transgressions and bruised for our iniquities (Isa. 53:5). *Iniquity* refers to the bending toward what is perverse or depraved.[1] We see again in Isaiah 32:6 the word *iniquity*, and it refers to the bending toward evil. Where sin may be the final action or result of iniquity, iniquity is the bent toward that sin. It is similar to an arrow that has not been straightened properly; the bend in the shaft will cause the arrow to miss the target. Missing the target is the very definition of sin. Therefore iniquities are tendencies toward sin and away from the target of righteousness in our lives. How many of us can see in our own lives and in the lives of our families the common bent toward particular sins? This shaping is passed down spiritually as much as it is genetically; I call it spiritual DNA. Whether it is environmental influences or spiritual influences—and in my opinion it is a combination of both—we can all see habits and patterns in our family line that lead to repeated sins and sicknesses generation after generation. These are our family alliances with the enemy. These are places of destruction and safe havens of sin that provide the enemy a refuge and hiding place from which he can operate in our own lives, marriages, and children's lives. It provides him with what Ephesians 4:27 calls "a foothold" (NIV). A foothold is a space that can be occupied or a place of significance. This is what our habitual sins give the enemy in our homes, an unnecessary place of significance.

Sisera turned to the tent of Jael because he thought he would have refuge there. He probably had previously experienced that refuge and hospitality in her home or the home of a member of her family. Jael and her family had always been a safe place for him, a friend to the enemy. When he was in trouble, he expected to find safety and a hiding place in her tent. That day was different, however, because there were no other family members present to intervene for the enemy. There was no one home but Jael, and she had determined that day that she had had enough. She had determined that the enemy would not be welcome in her tent any longer! She was loyal to God and the people of God, and no longer would she watch Jabin and Sisera enslave them. She knew the true authority and One to be feared was not Sisera or even Jabin. Her fear was in the Lord. This is the answer to a mother who may operate in a spirit of fear and intimidation. If we have the proper fear of the Lord, any fear of man will fade. Our desire to please Him will outweigh any temptation to please man. Jael did not fear Sisera because she feared God.

Jael had made up her mind that day that the family alliance, this generational iniquity, would stop with her. She refused to miss her target. It was just as the mighty warrior Shammah in 2 Samuel 23:11–12. Year after year the enemy stole the lentils of his family's garden. One year, however, something shifted inside of him. He said enough was enough. He was determined to defend his field of lentils even at the risk of his own life! That day Shammah broke the cycle over his family, and Jael chose to make the same shift. She was determined to break the cycle, and she said to herself, "I will not let the enemy do to me today what he has done to my parents and my grandparents and the generations before me." Jael fought so her children would not have to. She stopped accommodating or entertaining this enemy for the sake of their future!

CYCLE BREAKERS AND TENT SHAKERS

God is looking for some cycle breakers and tent shakers; He is looking for women who are more concerned with victory than stability. Jael was willing to risk the stability of her tent, her home, and her family structure in order to completely destroy the enemy that day. She was willing to use a tent peg from her own home to kill the enemy by driving it into his head (Judg. 4:21).

What if that tent peg was a corner of her house? Traditionally the women in nomadic tribes, such as the one Jael belonged to, helped to erect the tents. She had literally built this foundation with her own hands and secured those tent pegs. However, she looked beyond temporary stability for a lasting victory and pulled up a structure she had constructed herself and used it against her enemy.

What if defeating generational cycles and tendencies means we have to jerk up some false foundations we laid in our families? Many times breaking generational cycles causes a little temporary instability in our homes because we recognize that we have relied on a foundation that contains flaws and deception. We are forced to recognize lies that we have built our lives upon and even passed to our children. Truth brings freedom, but it also reveals what we at times do not want to see. Are we willing to see the truth it takes to experience true freedom in our home? What if it means our tent might shake a little bit in order to find true stability, but the shaking is necessary? Deliverance is not always neat and pretty, and victory over generational cycles sometimes requires shaking at the core. Woman of God, are you allowing the enemy to sleep in your tent to preserve temporary peace and a false sense of security? Or have you finally reached a place where you have had enough?

You, like Jael, are the only person who stands between your enemy and your children. Doing nothing is not an option. He has crossed the threshold of your home. The battlefield is no longer just in the middle of city squares or rough neighborhoods or political offices. The battlefield is in your house! The battlefield is in the airways of your home, on your television and your computers, on your children's electronic devices, and in the relationships your children form. You must realize the enemy will take any open door or foothold he can, no matter how big or small. What will you choose? To stand by and do nothing? To remain drowsy or distracted with the business of life?

Jesus said He would shake everything that could be shaken so that all that remains is of Him (Heb. 12:25–29). I fear some of us are far too concerned about stability of what has been to dare to aim for victory in future generations. The enemy has had access to your dwelling place long enough, and the Holy Spirit desires to evict him once and for all. It's time for our homes to be inhabited by the glory of God and His Spirit with no room for the enemy or his schemes.

THE POWER OF SUBMISSION AND OBEDIENCE

What weapons of warfare will you choose? How will you defeat the enemy at your door? There is no Deborah there to save you in the late hours of the night. There is no armed warrior guarding your tent in the middle of the afternoon. It is you and the Holy Spirit alone, and the Lord has set it up that way on purpose.

That was the arsenal of Jael. She never picked up a sword, and she never tried to use a spear. She would have never succeeded with a weapon she was not accustomed to; her enemy would have surely defeated her. Instead, she used the gift of hospitality and the kindness of her submissive spirit to lure him into a false sense of security. He never saw his fate coming. She was wise and fought with skillful strategy and with weapons with which she had experience. She used these weapons regularly in her everyday life.

Mom, don't deceive yourself into thinking that your gifts and abilities are not enough. You already have everything you need to win the victory against your adversary. Never underestimate what is in your hand just because it doesn't look like a weapon. Just look at Moses. He proved himself to Pharaoh and brought devastating plagues to Egypt and even parted the Red Sea with a simple shepherd's staff (Exod. 7–14). It was not a typical weapon of intimidation. The judge Samson took the jawbone of a donkey and slew one thousand Philistines (Judg. 15:15). David ran head-on toward the giant Goliath and only had the familiar tools of his shepherd's bag: stones and a sling (1 Sam. 17:49). It was hardly a reasonable defense against the mighty Goliath, yet Goliath fell before David. You too, Mom, should trust that the Lord has equipped you with everything you need to win the battle that is before you, and have confidence in the gifts He has given you.

It took some time, but Jael had the enemy right where she wanted him. She acted in the same manner as Esther. Esther had an enemy right in her home and in the ear of her husband. She never used a sword or even raised her voice. She fought her battles on her knees, and she used what she had been given to win the fight. She used her beauty and her submissive spirit to win the heart of the king to invite him to her strategic banquet. Then she also set a trap for her adversary with the gift of hospitality. She was patient and strategic and made her enemy feel at ease as she moved in for the kill. Jael also used her gift of hospitality to lure her enemy into her hands.

Our society underestimates the weapons of submission and meekness. Many think that to be meek is to be weak, but it is actually the opposite. It takes a greater strength to operate in restraint, especially when provoked. *Meekness* has been defined as "power under control."[2] Submission is when we choose to surrender or yield our authority to someone else. Deborah demonstrated the power of submission when she guided the battle from the passenger seat of the chariot. She didn't need control of the horse's reins

> It is you and the Holy Spirit alone, and the Lord has set it up that way on purpose.

or to be in charge. She accomplished her assignment right in her seat as she allowed Barak to lead. She was over him as judge but placed herself under him as he led in battle. There was no power struggle because Deborah did not fear submission. She was secure in her seat.

It is a heart of submission and obedience to the Lord that

will invite His presence and glory to reign in your home and truly make you dangerous in the Spirit.

Jael took up a tent peg that had been a foundation of stability of her home and struck it with a hammer, which represents the Word of God. The Word was not just a sword in this story, as we may traditionally think. It is a hammer. Jeremiah 23:29 says, "Is not My word…like a hammer that breaks rock in pieces?" Not only can the Word pierce, but the Word also has the power to break. It is the constant use of the Word that will turn strongholds into rubble. When dealing with generational strongholds and iniquities, we must apply the repetitive and consistent use of the Word, just like a hammer striking a rock. It may seem unproductive for the first few strikes, and the progress may be difficult to track. It may take a lot of effort and sweat and seem to not budge the rock. However, with every swing that rock or stronghold is actually being weakened from within. This is the power of the Word. Just keep swinging the Word, woman of God. It may take time and precision. You may get tired and at times be discouraged, but you are weakening the stronghold from within. In one moment the rock that seemed so unmovable will begin to break apart and shatter into pieces. This is the result of consistent, targeted use of the Word of God. Speak the Word over your children; post it in your home and on your mirrors. Read it aloud during the day, and pray it over your family members as they go to sleep. Swing the Word! It cannot and will not return void, according to Isaiah 55:11.

No longer will your family be held hostage by generational strongholds and alliances with the enemy! Rise up with me and declare, as Jael did, that what was allowed in your home before will no longer be allowed after today.

I declare determination and strength over you to hammer until your family is completely free from every alliance that has been created with the enemy. May every faulty foundation be uprooted. We release a shaking that will shake us free of every bondage and reestablish us in the truth that brings freedom. I declare that the Word will shatter what has taken the enemy generations to build. In the name of Jesus, that enemy is not welcome in your home anymore! ❖

Chapter Fourteen
THROW OFF THE
TASKMASTER SPIRIT

R ECENTLY GOD GAVE me one of those unique moments where He divinely interrupted my day to speak something life-changing to me. We as mothers are sometimes on the go so much that finding quiet time is a challenge. However, in His grace God understands motherhood. He will meet us where we are and get our attention in a way that only He can, letting us know that He is watching and is very much involved in every area of our lives.

I was walking out of my children's school, talking with another mom, when a sweet little bird flew over us at an abnormally low altitude. Something was wrong; she could not maintain height and sank to the ground beside us. My friend and I both stopped our conversation to take note of the struggle of this bird, as it would begin to fly up into the air, only to sink again. Over and over we watched it fail to take off. We knew it was not normal, and as we looked closer, we quickly realized what was taking place: the bird had a mouthful of building material for its nest. She was attempting to build a resting place for her babies, but the load she was carrying was too heavy to fly with. I knew the Lord was showing me a picture of myself, and I wanted to laugh and cry at the same time.

This little momma bird was trying with all her heart to

do what she thought was best for her babies. Her intentions were pure and unselfish. However, the load she was trying to carry at one time was too much for her. She was not built to soar with such a load. She kept trying to fly and kept sinking to the ground, and all the while she refused to release even the smallest portion of the load. All she had to do was let go and trust that what she could carry was enough, and she could have soared again. All the good intentions she may have had only put her in danger of being harmed on the ground and never reaching her babies at all.

"Why is she doing this?" I thought. Maybe she saw another bird who was bigger or stronger than her and thought she should be able to carry the same load. Maybe she forgot she was designed differently and bought into the lie of comparison. Maybe she thought bigger was better and was adding so much to her nest in such a little amount of time that she could not pace herself to build it little by little. Maybe she overloaded her schedule and her nest size thinking her babies needed more. Maybe she thought they would love her more if she could carry more and do more. Maybe she was an insecure mom seeking the approval of her children and affirmation from others in her house.

Spend your time on things that will last longer than that day, not just on the to-do list of the moment. Jesus gave you permission to do so!

The truth is those baby birds needed her more than they needed more padding on the nest. Why didn't this bird get it? For the same reason many of us don't: we think we can carry more than God designed us to carry. The heavy load that many mothers walk under only jeopardizes their health and spiritual safety, which, in turn, endangers the ones they are trying to serve. If you can't soar, you can't be the nurturer, provider, or example that your children need you to be. When you are weighed down, everyone suffers. You cannot sacrifice your ability to soar for doing what you have been deceived into thinking is best for your family. They need you to operate under the grace and capacity that God designed for you to carry. They need to see you soar, even if that means you must let go of some of the bells and whistles of life.

ETERNAL OR TEMPORAL INVESTMENT

This reminds me of the well-known story of Mary and Martha. Both women loved Jesus, but both had a very different perception of what He expected of them. In Luke 10 the Word says Jesus was traveling into the village (v. 38). This was what laborers and reapers did at the end of the day to seek food and rest from their labor. Jesus was coming to their house to relax and be refreshed. Mary and Martha each had a different interpretation of what Jesus wanted or needed when He stopped by, but Mary got it. She realized the important thing was to be at His feet in communion, not in the kitchen in service (v. 39). Sure, there is always a place to serve; we as moms live a life of service. However, serving cannot crowd out or replace our quiet times of intimacy with the Lord. Martha was upset that Mary did not work but spent time with Him (v. 40). I have experienced the Martha anger many times in my life, mostly directed toward my husband. He would always find time to play games with the kids or just sit and watch a movie while I was over at the sink scrubbing dishes or folding laundry. Instead of laying the work aside for a moment to be present with my family, I would get angry that he was not helping me accomplish my list of things to do. As my children have gotten older, I now realize that memories are not built on how many loads of laundry I washed for them or how many mornings their uniforms were pressed. They don't have any memory of which days the house was spotless and which days it was dirty. They remember the times I was present with them in intimate relationship. Those are the memories that last.

Jesus told Martha the same thing. What Martha had chosen to do with her time would fade as soon as the meal was done. What Mary had chosen would last a lifetime and could not be taken from her (Luke 10:42). It was not a temporal investment as was the serving of a meal, but it was an eternal investment. As you schedule your life and determine the daily load you will carry, remember the words of Christ, and spend your time on eternal, not just temporal, things. Spend your time on things that will last longer than that day, not just on the to-do list of the moment. Jesus gave you permission to do so! If only that little bird I saw had the knowledge of Scripture and knew the truth. God said in Matthew 6:26 that He watches the birds and is careful to feed them and take care of them. There was no need for this bird to carry the unnecessary load. The bird exhibited behavior that demonstrated it must have been ignorant of God and His care for her. Do our lives make us look disconnected from a Savior we can love and trust? Could someone watching us say, as Jesus did to Martha, "You are anxious and troubled about many things. But [only] one thing is needed" (Luke 10:41–42). Jesus was saying to quit complicating what is simple; His yoke is easy and His burden is light (Matt. 11:30). His expectations are not the same as yours, and what He expects from you He also supplies grace to accomplish!

THE SPIRIT THAT LEADS YOU

Mothers in our generation need to be released from what I call the taskmaster spirit. It is a demonic assignment to enslave you and shape your identity from tasks performed and accomplishments achieved. In the Book of Exodus the children of Israel were daily driven by taskmasters who used their strength and skill to build the wicked kingdom of Pharaoh (Exod. 1). The people of God worked and sweat, but they never enjoyed the fruits of their labor. This taskmaster spirit is still in operation with many of the children of God today. It's the taskmaster who will drive you to exhaustion and use you until you are spent for a purpose below that for which you were created. The taskmaster has the same voice of Martha, criticizing the mothers with a Mary heart.

Eve was a daughter with authority before she was ever a mother with responsibility. Your children need to see you be a daughter of God, passionately in love with Him.

It will always attempt to guilt or condemn you and taunt you every time to sit at the feet of Jesus. I release you, Mom, from the oppression of the taskmaster spirit, the oppressor that drives you. You are more than what you produce, and your role as a mother is not just as a servant and producer. You are also designed to lead and soar in your identity as a daughter of God.

You were a daughter before you were a mother, and I don't just mean in a physical sense. Before Eve was the mother of all, she was the daughter of One. In the garden she was first created as a daughter of God who reigned in codominion with Adam. Her name, *Woman*, was a name that connected her with Adam and denoted that she was a separate expression of the same being (Gen. 2:23). They were both Adam, and they both reigned in dominion. It was not until after the Fall, when Adam was given dominion over her, that her identity was changed. Sin changed woman's identity. Adam had been given the ability to name what he had dominion over in creation up until that point. After the Fall he was given the same ability to name woman as he named every other creature over which he had dominion. He changed her name to Eve, which meant "mother of all living" (Gen. 3:20).

There was an identity shift from coheir to producer. Her name identified what she could produce, but it did not encapsulate who she was originally created to be. She was a daughter with authority before she was ever a mother with responsibility. Being a mother was an honor, but it was not the fullness of her identity. When woman was first created, there were no children, and there were no dirty dishes! She was first created for communion with Adam and with God.

You, woman of God, are a daughter before you are a mother. Your identity cannot be wrapped up in what you produce. Your children need to see you soar in your identity beyond being their caretaker and need-meeter. They need to see you be a daughter of God, passionately in love with Him. When you seek Him first in this way, all the things you are trying to obtain and accomplish with your own efforts will simply be added to you. In other words, seek Him first, and He will gather the rest of the load for you (Matt. 6:33). Don't fear dropping the excess baggage you are carrying. Trust Him. He has you and your family in the safety of His care. Cast your cares on Him, and allow Him to care for you (1 Pet. 5:7). Don't look like the silly bird I saw who had no trust in her maker. Throw off the taskmaster mentality, and operate in kingdom grace. Be free from unnecessary weights and burdens, and demonstrate not only your mother side but also your daughter side. That is the eternal investment that Jesus said will not be taken from you.

I declare freedom and release over you, kingdom mother—first the freedom to soar instead of struggle, and then the courage to release the weight that is holding you back and weighing you down from soaring in the grace for your assignment. I declare that worry and stress to produce is leaving your life in Jesus's name. I pray for an identity shift over your life so you can lay aside every weight and distraction and place your focus on what is eternal and not just what is temporal. In the name of Jesus I break off the taskmaster spirit assigned to afflict you, and I declare that the Holy Spirit will lead you into revelation of being a daughter and sitting at Abba's feet. ❖

Chapter Fifteen
LEARN TO BURN

>>>———————————————◆

DARKNESS IS SO deceptive. It masks what is truly present and covers what is normally visible. Darkness simply hides everything that is easily seen or perceived in the light. It is no wonder that the enemy hides in darkness. It becomes a veil and camouflage for his schemes. This is why it is so important for a child of God to bring light into every dark place. Jesus commissioned us to be the light of the world (Matt 5:14). If we as the light truly saturated every city and nation, wickedness would no longer prevail. If light were to truly invade your home, the enemy would no longer have the convenience of being unnoticed as he attempts to divide and steal from your family. As kingdom mothers we must endeavor to cry out for light to dispel darkness, and that light must be released from within us!

What does it truly mean to be the light? What is so powerful about light that Christ would call Himself the light of the world (John 8:12) and commission us to be light? Light is such a powerful force that it doesn't even have to make a sound to make its presence known. It doesn't have to fight against darkness or struggle to make room for itself. When light appears, darkness dissipates. It flees. Light gives visibility and also emits warmth. It changes the state of the atmosphere by changing perspective and changing temperature. In the very beginning God spoke light as the backdrop to His creative ability (Gen. 1:3). Light was the canvas upon which the earth was created. It was a precursor to His Word going forth. Light set the atmosphere for His Word to bear fruit, and everything that God spoke came into being.

ILLUMINATE YOUR HOME

At the church Kevin and I pastor, we are so blessed to have a school of ministry not only for our adult students but also for the children of our church. Our elementary, middle, and high school students gather daily not only to accomplish their academic goals but also to be trained in the kingdom of God. Part of the curriculum requirements for our entire school is a class called Jewish Customs. I have always been obsessed with studying our Hebrew roots, and I love sneaking in to participate when our students celebrate the annual Jewish feasts. As I sat with my daughters at a Passover reenactment, God gave me one of the most profound revelations concerning my role as a mother and wife in my home.

As our class prepared to begin the Passover celebration, our teacher instructed us that the feast starts just as the weekly Shabbat starts, with the family gathered around the table in anticipation of the beginning of the feast. The mother would have generally been the one to prepare and clean the house and also prepare the meal for the celebration. This reminds me of how David in Psalm 23 said the Lord serves his soul: "You prepare a table before me in the presence of my enemies" (v. 5). The preparation is not always easy and may go unnoticed during the process, but the investment of time and love from the mother can be seen and experienced as what she has prepared becomes a gathering place and a foundation for the family to come together and receive the Hebraic blessing over their lives. Without the preparation by the mother, the family would have no gathering point.

This is part of your God-given purpose, Mom. You can produce the gathering point of your home. The heartbeat and central flow of life can come from something as simple as the family table. Can I just be old-fashioned for a moment in an attempt to revive the family table in our homes in this nation? I know schedules fight it and life seems to work against it, but there is something formative and indescribable that happens when a family pauses together to fellowship and share a meal. It was the pattern for discipleship in the Book of Acts; the people went from house to house and broke bread together, and the church grew daily (Acts 2:46–47). It is the table that is the gathering place for Communion, the setting Christ chose to give one of the most intimate revelations of Himself at the Last Supper. The venue He chose was not the synagogue or a crowded auditorium. It was the family table. God chose the revelation of a father with his family in depicting His greatest act of love toward us.

This can be a pattern of discipleship in our own homes. Even if pizza is passed from plate to plate or chicken nuggets become the centerpiece, I challenge you, Mom, to take time to produce a gathering place for your family in the midst of our hectic culture. Don't let the TV or cell phones be the center of mealtime. Take a moment to look at each member of your family eye to eye and share in unscripted conversation. Just see what can happen when you make time for those moments. There is an unpredictable but extremely valuable synergy that takes place when the entire family is together, every age gathered at the same table. Even if it's just once per week, as Shabbat is, make it a goal that takes priority. I pray for a revival of the family table in America.

After the matriarch or mother of the home prepares the table, the family waits for a ceremonial act that initiates every

Shabbat and every feast. Without this act the feast cannot begin. Without this act the blessing cannot be released. There must be the lighting of the candles before the meal begins. Just as God first created light before His Word was released in Creation, so a light must first be lit so the verbal blessing of the father or patriarch can be released over the family. The meal begins with a fire, and the family sits in darkness until the fire of the candle is burning. Who is commissioned with the responsibility and honor of lighting the Shabbat or festival candle? Who is the spark to begin it all? It is the mother. Without the fire of the mother the family sits in darkness. What is even more amazing is that these candles cannot be lit with a new flame or a match, but they are lit by a flame that is already burning. In other words, the mother must bring an existing burning flame to the table to start the fire. She must already be burning to bring light to her entire family.

At Passover that day at my children's school a flood of revelation overwhelmed me as I realized that we as mothers are responsible for being the fire starters in our homes. We have been commissioned to bring the light to the tables to prepare the way for the blessing of God over families. This light sets the atmosphere for the next tradition. The father or patriarch of the home places his hands upon the head of each of his children and releases a declaration of blessing over each member of his family. Just as God's prototype did in the beginning, the light establishes the atmosphere for the Word over the home, and one without the other is not complete. Mom, you are an atmosphere setter, and you are responsible for keeping the flame within you in order to keep the light burning in your whole house!

A woman on fire is the enemy's worst nightmare! If the

woman has an internal flame, she has the ability to light others upon contact. Fire is extremely contagious, and what it touches, it consumes. This means a group of women on fire could light an entire generation. It is no surprise that the enemy would work overtime to make sure the candle and flame of every mother is extinguished. It was his strategy in the beginning. When Satan purposed in his heart to steal the authority of the kingdom from Adam and Eve, he first set his efforts

> **Without the fire of the mother the family sits in darkness.**

upon Eve herself. She was the first matriarch and fire starter of humanity. Satan knew if he could gain the influence of Eve, she would, in turn, win Adam for him. He saw the gift of influence over the home that resided in her and decided to manipulate her into working on his team. The candle of man was extinguished by the influence of the woman.

This is the very reason for this Hebrew tradition of the woman's role in lighting the Shabbat candle. It is her job to redeem what she allowed to be extinguished. As the mother of the home lights the candle, not only is she setting an atmosphere for her family, but also she is sending a message to her adversary. It is an unspoken war cry and declaration of the woman to Satan; she is declaring that never again will she allow the enemy to use her influence to put out the candle of man. Instead, she will use her influence to ignite a flame against him!

Mothers, it's time to become flammable. It's time to be not only life givers but also *light* givers. But the first step in becoming a fire starter is to be on fire ourselves. Too many of us don't have the spark within us to light our homes, and our families are now sitting in the dark, and the blessing of God is being short-circuited. It is the Holy Spirit who is the original flame from the throne room of God, and He alone can start a fire within you. Jesus Himself is the Holy Ghost baptizer. John the Baptist declared that he would baptize in water, but the One coming after him (Jesus Christ) would baptize with the Holy Ghost and with fire (Matt. 3:11)! The Holy Spirit is not only about having a Pentecostal experience at the church altars. This gift of fire is about being flammable and spreading it wherever you go.

A woman on fire is the enemy's worst nightmare!

Once the disciples received the flame of the Spirit in Acts 2, they could not stay within the Upper Room where they had been praying. They had to go out and ignite others. They couldn't even stay within their city limits. What they received spread throughout Jerusalem, to Judea, to the uttermost parts of the earth, and that flame is still spreading across the earth today! This fire was never meant to be contained. It was meant to be contagious. Containing a fire is what will extinguish it. That is why Jesus said that you do not put a candle under a bowl. You set it on a table to share its light (Matt. 5:15). Mom, you need the continual burning flame of the Holy Spirit in your life, without containment and restriction. You can start a fire that cannot be contained.

I break limitations and the confinement of the enemy off of you and your calling! The enemy has tried to contain and restrict you so he can extinguish your flame. He has tried to suffocate your passion and silence your influence in an attempt to destroy your anointing, but I declare today that the enemy's boundary lines are breaking off of your life.

I pray that every assignment of the enemy to extinguish your spark and contain your flame would be exposed. I pray there would be an outpouring of the Holy Spirit upon you as in the Book of Acts and that a flame would sit upon you and consume you from the inside out. I pray that you would become combustible with His Spirit and presence and that house fires in the Spirit would break out across this nation and the nations of the earth. It's time to rise and shine, as Isaiah 60:1 admonishes us. And when you rise and shine, you will see that spiritual clarity comes to your home! It is the light that will make the path of God clear and provide direction. It is the light that will drive away confusion. It is the light that will illuminate what has been hiding in darkness so that you can see clearly to "clean house" and purify your dwelling place for the residing presence of the Holy Spirit. It is the light that will make way for the commanded blessing of the Lord.

FIND WHAT IS LOST

In Luke 15:8–10 Jesus tells a parable about a woman who had ten coins. She lost one in her own house. Each coin had value to her, and she was not satisfied with having only nine of them. She set out to turn her house upside down until she found what belonged to her! This parable is similar to the story of the good shepherd who left ninety-nine sheep to set out to find the one that was lost (Matt. 18:12–14). God is not appeased just by numbers of a crowd. As the Good Shepherd He never loses focus on the one, and mothers share in that same philosophy.

The Word says that the kingdom of God is like the coins, and I would submit to you that those coins can represent the children within your own home (Luke 15:10). They embody the kingdom. Just as this woman valued her coins, so you value your children. What do you do when something of value gets lost right under your nose, in your own house? I wonder how many of you reading this book have that one lost coin, that one son or daughter who carries such value to you but is lost right now. He may be just as this parable tells us, lost right in your own house—sitting in his bedroom, gathered at your table, but disconnected from God and from his purpose. He may be lost yet sitting on the pews of God's house. It is possible for one of your own to get lost despite the covering you provide for him. But this little lady would not give up until she recovered what was lost.

What was the solution for the lost coin? A lit candle and a broom (Luke 15:8). The Word says that this woman lit a candle over her house and began to sweep! She lit a fire that illuminated the junk that had hidden or buried her coin. What the light revealed she was diligent to sweep away and clean. The candle and the broom became the tools needed to recover the lost coin. These are the tools you need to use in the Spirit in your home, Mom. They are the same tools the woman of the home uses to prepare her house for Passover. She cleans out the junk and illuminates the darkness. As you allow the Holy Spirit to burn bright in you, you can light every dark place in your home that may be enveloping your children. The light will illuminate the dirt that has buried them so you can get it out of your house! Clean your house of compromise, carnality, and unrighteousness, and see if your lost coin doesn't begin to shine again.

The light pushed back the darkness so she could unveil her treasure! Her coin was there all along, but the absence of light in the home allowed her treasure to remain lost and hidden. Maybe there was some existing light, but it just wasn't bright enough to see into the hidden places of the home, and a greater light was needed. The absence of light allowed dust and dirt to pile up in her home, and they overtook her treasure. However, the presence of a flame brought redemption and allowed her to remove what was in the way! Her diligence was rewarded when what was lost was found!

For those of you who have lost coins in your house right now, I declare it's time to go on a treasure hunt! It's time to allow the Holy Spirit to set a fire in you that lights your whole house and illuminates wayward sons and daughters to salvation! I pray that an anointing to clean house in the Spirit would consume you and you would boldly dispose of all compromise, complacency, and carnality in your home. May the darkness flee at the presence of the Holy Spirit burning within you, and may all of your coins be found! ❖

Chapter Sixteen
DON'T EVER
LOSE YOUR PRAISE

⤜⟫⟩⟩▸————————————▸

USING EVERY WEAPON in your arsenal is necessary as you awaken the warrior within yourself. Different weapons are effective for different battles, and you must be led by the Spirit when deciding which weapon to unveil during a time of warfare. We have discussed some of these weapons already, but I want to take a few moments to address a very powerful weapon, one you must never let the enemy take from you during the heat of conflict. That weapon is your praise. It has the potential to turn the tide of battle in your favor. The weapon of praise is simple to use, and it is most effective when it is least expected by your adversary. It is a weapon made for a surprise attack.

GETTING LOST IN THE BATTLE

I learned the power of a praising mother during the birth of my fourth child, my daughter Judah. I had attempted natural birth for my first three children. I had a strong desire to experience labor as naturally as possible, but I had complications during my first three births that made natural delivery impossible. I gave up the thought of natural childbirth when I had to have a C-section with my daughter Zion, but the Lord in His mercy provided an obstetrician who allowed me to attempt what most would not: a natural delivery post C-section. I had determined that unless our lives were endangered, pain medication was not an option for me.

I did everything I could to prepare myself for my fourth delivery, but nothing would have adequately prepared me for the level of pain and agony I endured! Even though I had willingly chosen the path of natural delivery in the beginning, there still came a point when I wanted to quit, especially after I was given Pitocin to speed up and intensify my contractions. The pain was so overwhelming that I couldn't think clearly. I truly began to believe that I was going to die in this process and that no one around me, no nurse or doctor, even cared. It sounds silly now, but in my moment of struggle it was reality to me. This is what the battlefield can do to us sometimes. Distorted thinking and a clouded perspective can be the result of long-term struggle if we are not careful. Pain can alter our thinking, but pain is unavoidable in motherhood.

Becoming a mom is signing yourself up for heartache and struggle at times. Just the initial act of becoming a mother, giving birth, is one of the most intense processes of pain that a human being can experience. There are moments of unspeakable joy and peace and fulfillment, but the pressure can be overwhelming. There is not a pass card from battle or a get-out-of-pain-free card you can obtain through prayer. Even the most favored and honored mother in all of history, Mary, the mother of Jesus, was not exempt from heartache and pain. I am sure she found herself in spiritual battles that no one could have truly equipped her to encounter. In fact, it seems that the more prominent the purpose over a child and the more widespread his kingdom impact is designed to be, the greater the struggle and warfare that are surrounding his birth and development. Suffering was part of Mary's assignment as the mother of the Messiah. She was even told that a sword would pierce through her own heart when Jesus was just a tiny infant (Luke 2:35). That is not really the word of prophecy that we as mothers are looking for, but the truth is that every bundle of joy will bring with her a bundle of tests and trials and struggles.

PRAISING THROUGH THE BATTLE

The key to maintaining your victory and surviving the difficult seasons of motherhood is to never lose your praise. I learned this powerful lesson during my journey of natural birth. As I approached a personal breaking point in my labor with my daughter and truly thought my death was imminent, I asked my husband to pray for me. I was completely serious, but I think he was so shocked by my behavior during this phase of my labor and so unsure of my mind-set that he actually snickered at me as I cried out for prayer. I thought I was dying and cried out to God to have mercy on me, and he thought that was funny. Even while laughing, he faithfully prayed out loud for me. I actually had my arms wrapped around his neck as he completely supported me as I stood, a tactic to speed up labor. The nurses knew I was fading fast, and the only way out of this trial was to go through it as quickly as possible. So I held on to my husband's neck as he prayed, and he became my physical and spiritual support in that moment. I believe this unification of Kevin and me pleased the Lord; this is what God wills for the birthing of every season in our lives as parents. We needed each other in that moment, and we both shared in the pain of the struggle and the coming joy.

This is how the Son of God was born, with just Mary and Joseph in a stable. There was no nurse and no pain medication. It was just the two of them with all of heaven watching.

Joseph became her labor doula and shared in the struggle and joy alongside her. Similarly Kevin and I were petitioning heaven together, and much to our surprise the Lord spoke a word to us. "Deven," Kevin said. "The Lord actually just spoke to me a word for you. He said, 'Let praise come forth.'"

"What? Was this a cruel joke Kevin was playing on me?" I questioned. I was crying out for mercy and hurting so badly that I couldn't even breathe, and God was asking me to "let praise come forth." I was truly stunned for just a moment until the depth of what the Lord was saying was divinely revealed to me. Kevin and I had not been in agreement about the name of our daughter up until that point. I had felt the Lord whisper to me to call her Judah very early in my pregnancy, but Kevin had not yet received the same confirmation. As he spoke the word of the Lord to me in the delivery room, he was declaring her name with his own mouth without even realizing it. He was saying, "Let praise come forth," and *Judah* means "praise." The Spirit of God was declaring, "Let Judah come forth," and that is what happened both spiritually and naturally.

That moment of pain and struggle was the time for the weapon of praise to be released.

That moment of pain and struggle was the time for the weapon of praise to be released. God taught me a great lesson of motherhood that I still use as a reference point when I am in the midst of a battle or experiencing great pressure and struggle. I remind myself that right in that moment, when the enemy least expects it, is when praise is the most effective weapon. It carries the power and ability to shift our circumstances.

Praise shifted the walls of Jericho for Joshua. Praise shifted the battle for Gideon's outnumbered army. Praise shifted the prison where Paul and Silas had been shackled. Praise is a weapon that will shift things in your favor and take the enemy by surprise! In Judah's delivery room Kevin and I surrendered to the word of the Lord and unlocked the weapon of praise. As silly as we looked and sounded, and as difficult as it was to even muster the breath to speak, we began to release declarations of praise to the Lord. We praised Him with our voices, and we clapped our hands before Him. Instantly something shifted in that room and in my body. Within fifteen minutes Judah was delivered. As our praise came forth, Judah herself came forth. There was complete agreement on her name in that moment. The obedience of praise shifted my intolerable pain into unspeakable joy, and my tears of sorrow became tears of rejoicing. My deliverance was unlocked through my praise.

CHANGING THE ATMOSPHERE

Mothers, even in the heat of battle and during times of opposition you can never let the enemy silence your praise. Even when you don't think you have the strength to act in obedience to praise Him, you must reach down in your spirit and release your voice to give Him glory anyway. Like Paul and Silas, you must praise Him even when your arms are bound and your wounds are still bleeding. He is worthy in spite of our circumstances. A praising mother is a victorious mother. A home full of praise is a breeding ground for the glory of God.

When strife sets in, unleash the weapon of praise. When heaviness or sorrow clouds your home, unlock the weapon of praise. Become an atmosphere shifter by lifting your voice to the Lord because of His worth. Train your children to allow the praise of the Lord to continually be on their lips. It transforms them into potent weapons that shut the mouth of the enemy. Psalm 8:2 declares, "Out of the mouth of babes and nursing infants You have ordained strength because of Your enemies, to silence the enemy and the avenger."

I remember vividly one particular evening when the Wallace house was just full of strife. All four of my children were at each other's throats, and peace was far from us. A spirit of strife will invite all other types of darkness into your dwelling place, and it is something that we do not tolerate in the operating philosophy of our family. I had had enough, and the Spirit of the Lord prompted me to gather my children to shift the atmosphere. I called everyone into our living room, Kevin joined in, and I said, "We are going to corporately praise the Lord right now." The kids looked stunned and didn't quite take me or their father seriously at first. I gave further instruction and said, "I am serious, kiddos. We are going to change the atmosphere and the words of our mouth to please the Lord. We have invited strife in our home, but now we are going to invite His presence." I literally gave them no choice. If they had breath, they were commanded to use it. They could choose any of the seven methods of praise outlined in Scripture, but they had to praise Him.

Strife was broken in that moment, and the atmosphere was shifted. This is the power of praising parents and a praising family.

There was a brief moment of awkwardness, but Kevin and I just pressed right through it. I began to sing my praise to the Lord. My little girls joined in next. With all the sincerity of their hearts they began to clap and sing and shout before the Lord. Reluctantly the boys began to utter a few praises until they saw and felt the atmosphere shift. As they sensed something was happening in their hearts and over our home, they began to clap and shout even louder. Before I knew it, our entire family had lost our English to the heavenly prayer languages the Lord had given each of us, and we began to allow the Holy Spirit to make declarations over our home. Strife was broken in that moment, and the atmosphere was shifted. This is the power of praising parents and a praising family. It ushers in God's presence, and the enemy has no choice but to flee. This is a weapon that households across America need to utilize every day. May the airwaves of our homes be cleansed of all negative words, assignments of strife, and division. May our homes be saturated with words and music that invite the presence of the Lord to dwell with us and be glorified in the midst of our families. This will cause our children to grow deeper in God and our marriages to be unified and full of peace. Make an altar of praise right in the middle of your living room, and watch the true life of God flow throughout your family and shift the season of warfare over your home.

> I declare, Mom, that you will be silent no longer in your pain and struggle. I release the weapon of praise from your spirit that will take your enemy by surprise. I pray your soul would be reminded of the goodness of God and a declaration of His faithfulness would rise from within you. I declare the atmosphere of your home is shifting and the battle is turning in your favor. Let praise come forth, and watch God work on your behalf. ❖

Chapter Seventeen
ARISE AND SHINE!

‑‑≫≫»‑‑‑‑‑‑‑‑‑‑‑‑‑‑‑‑‑‑‑‑•

IDON'T KNOW HOW many of you wake your children up in the morning with the phrase "Rise and shine!," but I remember my mother often cheerfully declaring that phrase over me as she woke me up to get ready for school. I loved to sleep in and hated to hear those words! However, she loved me too much to leave me in my comfort. She knew I had somewhere important to be at a specific time, and if I didn't make it to school day after day, I could eventually ruin my future. Of course, none of that was running through my mind as I clung tight to my comfy pillow. I could only think of the moment. She, however, was thinking for my future.

RISE UP!

God, as our loving Father, responds to His sleeping children the same way. Isaiah 60:1–2 says, "Arise, shine, for your light has come, and the glory of the LORD has risen upon you. For the darkness shall cover the earth and deep darkness the peoples; but the LORD shall rise upon you, and His glory shall be seen upon you." I imagine in this text that the darkness of the world around His people must have lulled them to sleep, and they may have been comfortable in their complacency. You, Mom, may be in the same state: comfortable in a routine and only thinking for the moment; living in survival mode and clinging to your pillow of complacency, trying to drown out the voice of the Father. However, He is persistently calling His bride to arise.

That means we have to change our position. The command to arise puts responsibility on the one hearing and requires him to take action. Whatever is coming, whatever instruction is next, it cannot be done in the same position. It requires a change and significant movement. It requires us to transition from our comfortable state.

It is difficult to sleep standing up. As a teenager if I had continued to lie in my warm bed, even at the voice of my mother, I would have drifted back to sleep. It was a change from lying down to standing up that forced my body to alertness and began to set me in motion for my day. Her words carried value and authority, and I moved in response to them in obedience, even when I didn't feel like it. How much more should we honor the voice of the heavenly Father! However, that is not how many of us react to His commands. We hear His voice, but we never take the initiative to make a position change in our lives. We listen, yet we remain in a position of complacency. We hear His Word and His instruction, yet we return to our normal routines, never moving our lives and our schedules to accommodate what He is requiring. We become hearers of the Word but not doers. We naturally resist change. In the Spirit we remain in our warm beds, forget what He has spoken, and drift back off to sleep.

Awakening begins with His voice, but it can only continue in our lives if we react and make a position change. We have to recognize that whatever stance or position we have been in has allowed us to drift into spiritual slumber, and we cannot afford to remain asleep any longer. Similar to water that has become stagnant from sitting still too long, we need to be shocked into alertness and movement. The first step to shining and to lighting our home is to wake up and rise up in an intentional effort to hear the Word of the Lord in our lives. I pray the Spirit shakes us out of our beds and pushes us to our feet in attention to His Word!

Rising up can mean making a daily schedule change, such as making personal devotion in the Word of God and time for prayer and intercession a priority. I like to physically get up in the morning and light a candle in my home as a physical reminder to myself that I am setting an atmosphere for my family for the day. Rising up spiritually can literally mean rising up physically to seek Him. Rising up can be allowing regular times of not only prayer, but also prayer coupled with fasting to keep our spirits in tune with Him and to stand in the gap for the entire household. I have a dear friend who makes it a practice to fast once a month on the day of each of her children's birthdays. In other words, if her son's or daughter's birthday is on the fifteenth of the month, then she fasts every month on the fifteenth for that child. Fasting is not always a super spiritual feeling; it is a practice and a spiritual discipline. It is telling your flesh to wake up and listen to your spirit man! Like tuning our car radio in to our favorite station, fasting tunes our spirit to the frequency of heaven.

> *Whatever the Holy Spirit leads you to do, the important thing is to get up and actually do it!*

Rising up can mean making lifestyle changes in your home, such as having a weekly time for family dinner together and family devotion. It may mean you have to sweep out some things in your home to position your family for awakening. Maybe electronics need to be limited, or the TV needs to be limited daily instead of being the centerpiece of our homes. It may mean that you clean out the atmosphere of your home by cleaning the airwaves from ungodly music, ungodly conversations, and ungodly forms of entertainment. Whatever the Holy Spirit leads you to do, the important thing is to get up and actually do it!

SHINE!

Once we rise up, we become candidates to shine! It is interesting to note that in Isaiah 60:1–2 the prophet is calling the people of God to rise up when it is dark. In fact, it seems the darkness is the signal that it's time to get up! This is the opposite of our natural tendency. Our natural bodies were created to sleep at night and rise up at day, but in the Spirit it is the opposite. God created His bride to shine in darkness and thrive at night! In creation there are two types of creatures: nocturnal and diurnal ones. Diurnal creatures wake at the rising of the sun and function in daylight, but nocturnal creatures awaken as the night falls and thrive in darkness. They have special visionary tools and physical attributes made for the environment for which they were created. Those attributes would be wasted and ineffective in the daylight but work effectively and efficiently at night. A lightning bug in the sunshine is barely noticeable, but at night its beauty and purpose are clearly seen.

We as believers were created to be nocturnal in the Spirit. We may prefer the comfort of the day, but the truth is our skill set was created for the night. If we only shine when it's day, we are wasting our potential as vessels of the kingdom of God and the fire of the Holy Spirit. Just think about it. Who wastes their time to go watch a fireworks show in the middle of the day? It is just not effective because some things are just made for the night.

For this reason the bride of Christ should not give in to the temptation to run and hide as darkness envelops this earth. You should run toward it because you have been equipped to do something about it! Don't allow the darkness around you to lull you to sleep in your spirit. I pray it awakens you as the prophet Isaiah commands. You were made to shine in darkness!

There are specific nocturnal creatures known as bioluminescent creatures. They have a God-given ability to produce their own light in darkness. They literally have a chemical reaction within their bodies that causes them to glow. A firefly is the most well-known example of such a creature. You, Mom, were made to be a bioluminescent woman. Just as God's presence in the Old Testament transitioned from a cloud by day to a pillar of fire by night, so you should burn bright when darkness sets in around you. Your light should not dim when humanity's light dims because your light is not of this world; it comes from within.

With the fire of the Holy Spirit burning within you, you have the ability to produce your own light when you are placed in the dark. You do not have to depend on external sources or other individuals to keep your fire burning bright because your fuel source resides with you continuously. Your children are meant to be spiritually bioluminescent alongside you! In this dark hour it is time for you and your whole house to rise and shine with a light from within. Then the whole world will see the light and be drawn to Him.

I declare a movement across our nation and our globe. I declare a moms' awakening. May the Lord shake His bride, and may we as mothers rise and shine in this hour. May our light recover what has been lost in this generation. May we teach our children to shine with the fire of His presence. I declare a move of His Spirit will sweep the earth again, and may it start in your home. You are the key, and God is calling your name. It is time, Mom, to rise up and shine. ❖

Conclusion

‣⟫⟩⊶————————⊷

I PRAY THAT AS you have immersed yourself in the pages of this book, your spirit has been shaken and awakened to your kingdom assignment as a mother. I pray that you have heard the heartbeat of the Spirit for you and your entire household. We are indeed navigating our families through one of the most challenging times in our world, a time filled with depravity and darkness, and it almost doesn't seem fair at times to be raising children in such adverse circumstances. There is such an agenda for our culture to mold our children to a form that does not match the identity of Christ and the image of God they were created to display, both inwardly and outwardly. Instead, the assignment is to mold them to the idols of this world and ultimately to align them with the spirit and assignment of the antichrist, which has been at work in the world since the time of Christ (1 John 4:3).

To the parents of this generation, the pressure seems unbearable. It would be easy to become gripped with fear and anxiety. You may think the way I once did and try to determine how you can lock your doors and windows to keep your precious little ones from the big, bad world around them. However, this is the exact opposite of the heart of the Father for His people in this hour. This is exactly what the enemy wants to happen. He wants to intimidate you into hiding your light and disconnecting from the world around you.

Jesus's prayer for us, recorded in John 17, reflects His heartbeat. He does not pray that His followers would be taken out of this world (v. 15). His desire was for our presence to be here to complete the work He did for us on the cross. He passed the assignment to us to bring His kingdom to the earth. Jesus just said not to be of the world, meaning we cannot blend in or conform to it. We are the salt that flavors and the leaven that changes the whole lump! We are the mustard seed that spreads. These are all of the parables that Christ taught about the potency of our presence here. We have to be present to make an impact, but we have to be pure and undefiled to change the environment around us.

Many mothers are probably already developing a plan for their family to shine, but you may be approaching it in the wrong manner. You may already be frantically creating a list of what you need to change and your strategy for preparing your family spiritually, and a sense of panic may be enveloping you. After all, as a mom don't you already have enough on your to-do list? Let me remind you, you were never purposed to accomplish this alone. I used to strive for perfection, but all my work only drove to me exhaustion and despair. My victory came not in my efforts but in daily surrender. In a time when I thought I could please Him and accomplish more with all my spiritual activity, He was challenging me to rest in Him.

Rest, while rare for most mothers, is actually a very powerful weapon. We need rest both physically and spiritually. Your spirit was created for periods of rest, but never sleep. Sleep is to be in an unconscious and unaware state, but rest is simply to be motionless, free from labor and anxiety. Rest is a worry-free zone that can only be found in Christ. The purpose of this book is to awaken your spirit as a mother, but it is not to drive you to tireless work to achieve what you can only accomplish by the Spirit. We have to wake up from slumber but never lose a place of rest in Christ.

It all goes back to the revelation we discussed about the creation of woman. We were created for communion. Woman's first role each day was walking and talking with God in the garden and beside Adam. This is still God's design for you. Yes, in the unit of the family we have all been given strategic gifts and abilities to keep order and functionality. Dishes must be washed, and the laundry needs to be folded. However, there is a problem when our identity gets wrapped up in our performance, and our purpose rests in our daily tasks.

Mothers, let me challenge you to make eternal investments every day instead of just temporal ones. Don't just let your days be consumed with physical efforts of service to your family. Give yourself and your family something that is an investment that the enemy cannot steal and that will not fade. Just a moment of communion with the Lord can change your life and family.

I have to admit that at times I would resist the call to spend time with the Lord. I could be in the middle of laundry or working through a project for my job when the Lord would call my name for prayer. As mothers we are accustomed to hearing our names called over and over throughout our days. Most of the time when we hear our names, we know it is because someone we love needs something from us, and we spend the majority of our day giving of ourselves. However, God, unlike the many others in your life, is not calling on you to get something from you. He is calling you to give something to you. He shows up to recharge you and refresh you in His presence. He wants to give you rest in Him. Rest is the only way to ensure you can burn bright for your family and for the kingdom instead of burning out! The most effective way we can war for our children is from a place of spiritual rest, even when a storm is raging.

Your greatest weapon and your most important priority as a mother is the weapon of intimacy with the Father. This is the key to kingdom-minded parenting, supernatural fruit in your home, and victory in every battle. Discipline your life to seek Him in intercession and worship.

This is my prayer for you as a kingdom-minded mother: I pray that as you close the last pages of this book, you don't lay it down and take up fear or worry or feelings of insufficiency. Instead, take up a lifestyle of prayer like never before. I pray that you shake off carnal wisdom, worldly thinking, and idols that have consumed your time and heart, and you rise in an anointing to change the world through the seed in your own home. May an insatiable desire to pursue His presence and glory overtake you, and may you find your greatest victories in the war room of your prayer closest. I pray in those strategic times that divine parenting strategies, unique to your house, come to you. I pray that you will begin to see supernatural fruit in the lives of your precious little ones and that your entire house will begin to illuminate His kingdom. I declare that you will be full of the fire of His Spirit and walking in tune with His heartbeat in this hour.

This is how the warrior within you will rise up. This is how you will become the mighty archer He created you to be. Every time you bend your bow, hell will shake. Your adversary will see that you have shaped, sharpened, aimed, and ignited by the leading of the Holy Spirit. Hell will know that your arrows cannot and will not miss! This is what our nation and our world need—an awakening of the warriors to turn and awaken the prophetic voice of their sons and daughters, releasing them as fiery arrows into the darkness. Your fiery arrows, Mom, are sitting at your dinner table and riding in the backseat of your car every day. They are waiting on you to awaken to your purpose so they can be aligned to theirs. Like Hannah, Mary, Elizabeth, and Jochebed, you are the one the enemy should fear, for you are the one who houses the secret weapons of the kingdom. Let there be an awakening of the warrior we call mom, and let the hand that rocks the cradle shake the world for His glory.

NOTES

INTRODUCTION

1. "Gang Member Statistics," Statistic Brain, February 28, 2016, accessed October 27, 2016, http://www.statisticbrain.com/gang -statistics/.

2. "Suicide Prevention," Centers for Disease Control and Prevention, March 10, 2015, accessed October 27, 2016, http://www.cdc .gov/violenceprevention/suicide/youth_suicide.html.

3. Kalman Heller, "Depression in Teens and Children," Psych-Central, accessed November 29, 2016, http://psychcentral.com/lib /depression-in-teens-and-children/.

4. "Child Sexual Abuse Statistics," National Center for Victims of Crime, accessed October 27, 2016, https://victimsofcrime.org/ media/reporting-on-child-sexual-abuse/child-sexual-abuse -statistics.

5. Ross Toro, "Prescription Drug Abuse Kills," LiveScience, December 12, 2011, accessed November 29, 2016, http://www .livescience.com/17406-prescription-drug-abuse-infographic.html.

6. "Child Trafficking Statistics: U.S. & International," Ark of Hope for Children, March 19, 2016, accessed October 27, 2016, http://arkofhopeforchildren.org/child-trafficking/child-trafficking -statistics.

CHAPTER TWO
THE ARROWS IN YOUR QUIVER

1. "Lexicon::Strong's H5828—*ezer*," accessed December 2, 2016, https://www.blueletterbible.org/lang/lexicon/lexicon.cfm?Strongs =H5828&t=KJV.

CHAPTER THREE
BE LOOSED TO LEAD

1. William Ross Wallace, "The Hand That Rocks the Cradle Is the Hand That Rules the World," accessed December 2, 2016, http://www.potw.org/archive/potw391.html.

2. "What Was the Significance of Weaning a Child in the Bible (Genesis 21:8)?" Got Questions Ministries, accessed December 2,

2016, https://gotquestions.org/weaning-child-Bible.html; "Infant and Child Care," The Jewish Agency for Israel, August 28, 2005, accessed December 2, 2016, http://www.jewishagency.org/life-cycle /content/24257.

CHAPTER FOUR
KEEPING YOUR CHILDREN ON COURSE

1. Merriam-Webster, s.v. "reset," accessed November 2, 2016, http://www.merriam-webster.com/dictionary/reset.

CHAPTER FIVE
RAISING "LEFT-HANDED" WARRIORS

1. "Lexicon::Strong's H334—'itter," accessed December 5, 2016, https://www.blueletterbible.org/lang/lexicon/lexicon.cfm?Strongs =H334&t=KJV.
2. Richard Gottheil, Kaufmann Kohler, Marcus Jastrow, Louis Ginzberg, and Duncan McDonald, "Benjamin," Jewish Encyclopedia, accessed December 5, 2016, http://www.jewishencyclopedia .com/articles/2947-benjamin.

CHAPTER EIGHT
STOP COPING, AND START SHAPING

1. Yuritzy Ramos, "College Students Tend to Change Majors When They Find the One They Really Love," *Borderzine*, March 15, 2013, accessed December 6, 2016, http://borderzine.com/2013/03 /college-students-tend-to-change-majors-when-they-find-the-one -they-really-love.
2. Susan Adams, "Most Americans Are Unhappy at Work," *Forbes*, June 20, 2014, accessed December 7, 2016, http://www .forbes.com/sites/susanadams/2014/06/20/most-americans-are -unhappy-at-work/#335b3eab5862.
3. "Suicide Prevention," Centers for Disease Control and Prevention.
4. Charlie Kluge, *The Tallit: Experience the Mysteries of the Prayer Shawl and Other Hidden Treasures* (Lake Mary, FL: Charisma House, 2016), 103.

Chapter Ten
Mastering Release

1. "Lexicon::Strong's H286—*towb*," accessed December 15, 2016, https://www.blueletterbible.org/lang/lexicon/lexicon.cfm?Strongs =H2896&t=KJV.

2. "Lexicon::Strong's H1573—*gome*," accessed December 15, 2016, https://www.blueletterbible.org/lang/lexicon/lexicon.cfm ?Strongs=H1573&t=KJV.

3. Carolyn Roth, "Moses and the Bulrush Cradle," *God as a Gardener* (blog), August 6, 2011, accessed December 15, 2016, https://godasagardener.com/2011/08/06/moses-and-the-bulrush -cradle.

Chapter Eleven
Clothe Them; Don't Control Them

1. "Lexicon::Strong's H4598—*m@'iyl*," accessed December 12, 2016, https://www.blueletterbible.org/lang/Lexicon/Lexicon.cfm ?strongs=H4598&t=KJV.

2. James D. Strong, *The New Strong's Expanded Exhaustive Concordance of the Bible* (Nashville: Thomas Nelson, 2001), s.v. "*m*^*ec*^*iyl*."

Chapter Twelve
Be Fierce, Not Afraid

1. "Lexicon::Strong's H5828—*ezer*," accessed December 12, 2016, https://www.blueletterbible.org/lang/lexicon/lexicon.cfm?Strongs =H5828&t=KJV.

Chapter Thirteen
Breaking Generational Cycles

1. "Lexicon::Strong's H5771—*'avon*," accessed December 12, 2016, https://www.blueletterbible.org/lang/lexicon/lexicon.cfm ?Strongs=H5771&t=KJV.

2. Grady Scott, "Blessed Are the Meek," Bible Topics in the Christian Library, accessed December 12, 2016, http://www .christianlibrary.org/authors/Grady_Scott/matt5-5.htm.

Pastor Deven Wallace copastors Redemption Point Church with her husband, Bishop Kevin Wallace. She is the founder of The Zion Project, a nonprofit organization dedicated to abolishing human trafficking and empowering women and children to walk in their kingdom position. Her mandate is to rescue victims of abuse and empower them to break the silence. Deven is fueled with vision to mobilize people with a message of hope and restoration and to set the captives free. Deven has a prophetic message burning within her for people around the world to awaken to what God is doing. Her messages are causing a wave of revival and God's glory to be released in the nations of the earth.

Pastors Kevin and Deven live in Chattanooga, Tennessee, with their four children: Jeremiah, Isaiah, Zion, and Judah.

THE ZION PROJECT is a faith-based nonprofit organization with a focus on restoring women and children spiritually, physically, socially, financially, and emotionally. We strive to achieve holistic restoration of young women who are survivors of sexual exploitation and violence. Also, through awareness, we desire to create prevention for those who are at a high risk of becoming involved in this injustice. These goals are accomplished through education, exposure, restoration, and transformation. Currently The Zion Project has operations in the United States, Guatemala, Romania, Bulgaria, and Thailand. Some of The Zion Project's ongoing initiatives include Restoration Day Program, Hope Mentorship, Christmas Express, Beautifully Broken, and Education & Awareness assemblies with schools, churches, and civic organizations. The Zion Project's future plans include a Restoration Resource Center and Home in Southeast Tennessee.

RESTORING IDENTITY. RENEWING INTIMACY. RECLAIMING INHERITANCE.

WWW.THEZIONPROJECT.NET

CONNECT WITH US!

CHARISMA HOUSE

(Spiritual Growth)

f Facebook.com/CharismaHouse

🐦 @CharismaHouse

📷 Instagram.com/CharismaHouse

SILOAM

(Health)

📌 Pinterest.com/CharismaHouse

MODERN
ENGLISH
VERSION

(Bible)
www.mevbible.com